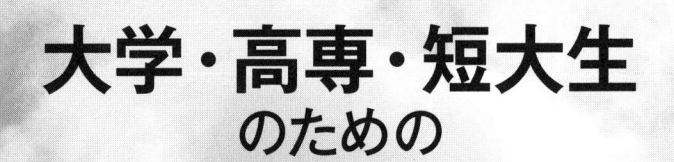

大学・高専・短大生
のための
英文法
再入門

桑本裕二
[監修]

桑本裕二　菅原隆行　中村弘子
二本柳譲治　福士智哉　福光優一郎
[著]

開拓社

はしがき

　昨今，英語教育の現場では「使える英語」というものが求められている．そして，本質を見極めないまま，「使える英語の養成」→「英語だけを使った授業」といったような短絡的な解釈がまかり通り，最近始まった小学校英語をはじめ，中学，高校，大学等における英語教育においては，学習者に十分に「使える英語」を養成してきたとはいいがたい．そうなってしまった主要な理由のひとつとして，文法理解，教授の軽視ということが挙げられる．音声刺激と身振り手振りによって，文法は適当でいいから，細かい部分の理解はどうでもいいからと，とにかく慣れさせることが全てであるとでも言わんばかりに，おしゃべりの延長のような授業を展開した結果，英語による正確な表現の全体像がつかめなくなってしまっている．

　英文法をしっかり知らないで英語を理解しようとするのは，例えばスポーツを，ルールを知らないで，また用具の使い方を知らないで，いきなりプレーさせられるようなものである．この場合に，もしそのスポーツの指導者が，「私がやるのを見て，やり方を身につけて下さい」などと言ったとしたらどうだろうか？それが効果的な指導法と言えるだろうか？また，習う側は，そのスポーツの技術をしっかりと身につけることができるだろうか？

　高等専門学校では，高等学校の全日制の学齢である1～3年次にすでに専門教育が開始される反面，英語等の人文系科目の教育が手薄になってしまっている．一方，5年間の在学期間を終えて就職するときには，かなりの英語力が望まれ，その対応は学生側も教師側も大変な努力を強いられるという現状である．その際に望まれるのは，たわいもない会話ができることではなく，論理的に筋道の立った，交渉術をともなった会話力であり，こみいった内容を適切に表現できる読解力と作文力（論文作成力）である．これは，4年制大学や2年制の短期大学にもそのまま当てはまる．

　本書は，一度は初等英文法を学び終わった大学1，2年次，短大，高等専門学校4，5年次の学生を対象に，英文法をもう一度，ただし，異なる視点で再確認し，理解を確かなものにすることを目指したものである．本書の執筆者のほとんどは，高等専門学校で実際に英語を教えた経験があり，基礎英文法を効果的に教授することの難しさを熟知し，自ら実践してきた経験を有する一方

2

で，大学や短大の基礎英語教育に携わり，同じく基礎力養成の困難に直面して
きた者もいる．また執筆者の中には，高校と高専，高専と大学，短大と大学と
いう異なる教育機関での教授の経験もあって，英文法の基礎知識の教授から，
応用，実践への連動的な指導の心得があり，やはり，実際に経験してきている．
このような執筆者たちがそれぞれ専門の研究分野の立場から，標準的な基礎英
文法の枠組みに沿いつつも，独自のとらえ方でそれぞれの文法項目を効果的に
説明していくというスタイルをとっている．

　本書は，このように，大学，高専，短大という高等教育機関での使用を意図
しているが，同じ目的で，高等学校，高校生向け学習塾，大学受験予備校での
参考図書としても十分に生かすことができるものと自負している．

　なお，本書執筆に際しては，以下の文献を参考にした．

江川泰一郎 (1982) *A New Approach to English Grammar.* 東京：東京書籍．

江川泰一郎 (1991)『英文法解説』東京：金子書房．

綿貫陽他 (2000)『改訂新版　ロイヤル英文法』東京：旺文社．

宮川幸久他 (2010)『[要点明解] アルファ英文法』東京：研究社．

Quirk, Randolph, Sidney Greenbaum, Geoffrey Leech, & Jan Svartvik (1985) *A Comprehensive Grammar of the English Language.* London and New York：Longman.

　編集，出版に際しては，開拓社出版部長川田賢氏に大変お世話になった．特
に，原稿脱稿が大幅に遅れてしまい，迷惑をかけてしまったことは慚愧に堪え
ない．

　また，英文校正には，Emily M. Bender（ワシントン大学教授），Tomek
Ziemba（大分工業高等専門学校一般科文系助教），Sean Banville（鳥取大学非
常勤講師），Gilbert G. Gallays（一関工業高等専門学校非常勤講師），Chris
Wolf（新居浜工業高等専門学校非常勤講師），他 1 名の方々にお世話になった．
記して謝意を表する次第である．

2018 年 9 月

編著者

目　次

はしがき・・ 2

第1章　Be・・・ 6

第2章　自動詞と他動詞・・・・・・・・・・・・・・・・・・・・・・・・・・・・・・・・・・ 10

第3章　主語と述語（動詞）・・・・・・・・・・・・・・・・・・・・・・・・・・・・・ 14

第4章　動詞の時制（1）・進行相・完了相・・・・・・・・・・・ 18

第5章　進行相・・・ 22

第6章　完了相・・・ 26

第7章　名詞と冠詞・・・・・・・・・・・・・・・・・・・・・・・・・・・・・・・・・・・・・・・ 30

第8章　代名詞・・・ 34

第9章　前置詞・・・ 38

第10章　形容詞と副詞・・・・・・・・・・・・・・・・・・・・・・・・・・・・・・・・・・・・ 42

第11章　関係詞（1）　関係代名詞・・・・・・・・・・・・・・・・・・・・・ 46

第12章　関係詞（2）　関係副詞等・・・・・・・・・・・・・・・・・・・・・ 50

第13章　関係詞（3）　その他の応用的用法・・・・・・・・・・・ 54

第14章　まとめ（1）　文の種類・・・・・・・・・・・・・・・・・・・・・・・ 58

第15章　句と節・・・ 62

第16章　接続詞と文の接続・・・・・・・・・・・・・・・・・・・・・・・・・・・・・・ 66

第17章　不定詞（to 不定詞・原形不定詞）・・・・・・・・・・・・・ 70

第18章　分詞（現在分詞・過去分詞・分詞構文）・・・・・・・ 74

第19章　動名詞・・・ 78

第20章　比較表現・・・ 82

第21章　受動態・・・ 86

4

第22章	使役構文	90
第23章	助動詞の表現	94
第24章	動詞の時制 (2)	98
第25章	仮定法 (1)	102
第26章	仮定法 (2)	106
第27章	話法	110
第28章	まとめ (2) 5文型	114

執筆者紹介 · · · · · · · 118

覚えておきたい 英単語

1	国名・地名	9	15	国際問題	65
2	町の施設など	13	16	文具類など	69
3	交通・通学（通勤）	17	17	事務処理・面接	73
4	観光・出張・旅行	21	18	書籍・出版・学術論文	77
5	行政・市民生活	25	19	銀行・金融	81
6	福祉・保険	29	20	差別・平等	85
7	政治	33	21	和製英語のもとの英語	89
8	病院・病気・症状	37	22	重要な形容詞・副詞	93
9	不動産・賃貸契約	41	23	まぎらわしい綴りの組〈1〉	97
10	自動車	45	24	同綴異義語	101
11	社会問題・犯罪	49	25	対義語の対	105
12	企業・会社	53	26	同音異義語	109
13	職場・オフィス	57	27	まぎらわしい綴りの組〈2〉	113
14	配達・輸送	61	28	まぎらわしい綴りの組〈3〉	117

第**1**章　Be

be の意味

be: 〜である，〜がいる（ある）

　動詞 "be" は，「〜である」「〜がいる（ある）」などのように訳され，状態，存在などを表現するのに用いられる．"be" を使った文の，"be" の前の部分（主語 S）と後ろの部分（補語 C）は等価のものとみなされ，**連辞**（**copula**）とも呼ばれる．

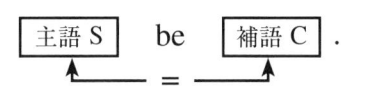

John	is	a teacher.	（名詞句）	「ジョンは先生です．」
		clever.	（形容詞句）	「ジョンは賢いです．」
		in the living room.	（前置詞句）	「ジョンはリビングにいます．」
		here.	（副詞句）	「ジョンはここにいます．」

進行形と受動態の be

　進行形 "be 〜 ing" は，"be" の補語として現在分詞「〜している」をとったものが，受動態の "be＋過去分詞" は，"be" の補語として過去分詞「〜される」をとったものが，それぞれ文法化したものと解釈できる．

（現在）進行形（be＋現在分詞）

　John　is　studying now.
　「ジョンは今勉強中です．」

受動態（be＋過去分詞）

　John　is　known as a famous musician.
　「ジョンは有名なミュージシャンとして知られています．」

6

■ 存在文

There is (are) 〜.「〜がある（いる）」

存在文「〜がある（いる）」は，"There is [名詞単数形]." "There are [名詞複数形]." で表現される．

There ｜ is ｜ ｜ a book ｜ on the desk.
　　　　　　　　名詞単数形

There ｜ are ｜ ｜ some pieces of cake ｜ in the dish.
　　　　　　　　名詞複数形

"There is/are 〜." の構文は，疑問文では先行する "there" と "be" の位置がひっくり返るが，"be" の活用は後続の名詞句に従う．

存在文の疑問文

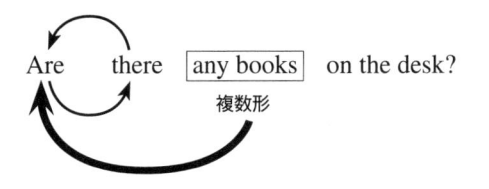

Are　　there ｜ any books ｜ on the desk?
　　　　　　　　複数形

■ 活用形

"be" の述語動詞（文の動詞）は，現在形は "am" "are" "is" の3形，過去形は "was" "were" の2形に活用するが，以下のとおり，人称，数に応じて6種類の主語に対応しているととらえるべきである．

"be" の現在活用形（現在形（present））

	単数 (singular)	複数 (plural)
一人称	I am	we are
二人称	you are	you are
三人称	he/she/it is	they are

"be" の過去活用形（過去形（past））

	単数 (singular)	複数 (plural)
一人称	I was	we were
二人称	you were	you were
三人称	he/she/it was	they were

7

Exercise 1

1. 次の to 不定詞句について，人称（一人称／二人称／三人称），数（単数／複数）に基づいて現在形を 6 種類に活用させ，それぞれ文を作りなさい（三人称単数／複数の主語はそれぞれ "he" "they" にすること）．

1) to be young
2) to be a teacher/teachers
3) to be running along the river
4) to be known to every student in the college

2. 次の to 不定詞句について，人称（一人称／二人称／三人称），数（単数／複数）に基づいて過去形を 6 種類に活用させ，それぞれ文を作りなさい（三人称単数／複数の主語はそれぞれ "he" "they" にすること）．

1) to be clever in one's school days
2) to be an actor/actors ten years ago
3) to be learning English in this elementary school
4) to be spoken to on the street suddenly from behind

3. それぞれの文を疑問文に直し，日本語に訳しなさい．

1) There are some pieces of paper on the desk.
2) You were a doctor before.
3) Masao is designing his own web site now.
4) I am Momotaro in the play.

4. それぞれの文（3）は下線部）を否定文に直し，日本語に訳しなさい．

1) You are older than James.
2) He was stupid enough to do such a thing.
3) I am Indian, so I can't understand what people in any cities were talking about during my trip in India.
4) The digital camera was in the drawer of my office desk then.

5. それぞれの日本文を英語に訳しなさい.
   1) その本は確かにこの部屋にあったが，今はない．（確かに：certainly）
   2) なにか質問ありますか？
   3) エミリーはさっきここにいましたよ．

覚えておきたい
英単語　**1** 国名・地名

アメリカ合衆国／アメリカ人	The United States of America / American(s)
中国／中国人	China / Chinese
韓国／韓国人	Korea / Korean
台湾／台湾人	Taiwan / Taiwanese
イギリス／イギリス人	England / English
フランス／フランス人	France / French
ドイツ／ドイツ人	Germany / German(s)
ロシア／ロシア人	Russia / Russian(s)
スペイン／スペイン人	Spain / Spanish
イタリア／イタリア人	Italy / Italian(s)
インド／インド人	India / Indian(s)
オーストラリア／オーストラリア人	Australia / Australian(s)
アラビア／アラビア人	Arabia / Arab(s)

第2章 自動詞と他動詞

意味上の区別

動詞の意味を考えた場合，その動作が，動作をおこすもの自体に関わる場合，その動詞を**自動詞**（**intransitive verb**）という．

自動詞の例：walk, stand, run, stay, go, come, …

Tom walks along the river every morning.

動作をおこすもの

これに対し，eat「食べる」のように，その動作を表現する場合に，動作を起こすもの（「食べる」動作を行うもの）の他に，動作がおよぶ対象（「食べる」対象の食べ物）が必要な場合，その動詞を**他動詞**（**transitive verb**）という．

他動詞の例：eat, have, like, catch, make, …

Japanese people eat rice as a principal food.

動作をおこすもの　動作がおよぶ対象

構文上の区別

構文上は，上記の「動作をおこすもの」は，受動態でなければ文の**主語**（**subject**）になる．「動作がおよぶ対象」は，**目的語**（**object**）となる．つまり，構文上は，自動詞は主語のみ必須で，他動詞は主語と目的語が必須となる．

自動詞の例：

The train stopped suddenly in front of the bridge.
S（主語）　V（動詞）

他動詞の例：

Today's students use their electronic dictionaries in class.
S（主語）　　V（動詞）　　O（目的語）

10

自動詞・他動詞のいろいろ

"start" "stop" "write" "speak" "believe" "think" などは, 同一語形で自動詞／他動詞の両方の場合が可能である.

The Christmas party will start at 18:00 at my grandmother's house.

(start「始まる」[自動詞])

The bookstore started on-line ordering last September.

(start「始める」[他動詞])

前後関係により, または常識的に目的語が省略されて, 他動詞が自動詞のようにふるまう場合がある.

Our family often eat out on Sundays.　　　(eat out「外食する」[自動詞])

We must come in to our office next Sunday. — I know.

(I know (it). "it" の省略)

'Tis better to have loved and lost than never to have loved at all.

(Tennyson, *In memoriam*. love「愛情をそそぐ」(自動詞))

以下のものは, 本来的に他動詞／自動詞だったものが, 多少意味を変えて自動詞／他動詞に派生したものである.

The CDs of this famous idol singer sold well this year.

(sell「売る」(他動詞) → 「売れる」(自動詞))

Ms. Ito has been running this cosmetic company since its establishment.

(run「走る」(自動詞) → 「経営する (＜走らせる)」(他動詞))

まぎらわしい自動詞・他動詞

"visit"「訪問する」などは, 自動詞である "go"「行く」とほぼ同じ意味であるとみなしてしまい, いかにも自動詞のように感じられるが, 「～を訪問する」と解釈でき, 訪問する先を目的語にとる他動詞である. ほかに, "discuss"「～について議論する」も "discuss about ～" とするといかにも正しいようであるが, これは間違いで, 直接に目的語を取る他動詞である.

11

Lucy visited Tokyo twice in her college days.

Now, let's discuss several problems about the aftermath of the big earthquake.

また逆に，"look" "consist" などは，「～を見る」「～を構成する」と解釈され，いかにも他動詞のようであるが，それぞれ "look at ～" "consist of ～" のように前置詞を伴わないと意味をなさないので形の上では自動詞である．

Please look at the blackboard.

Exercise 2

1. 次の各文の下線部の動詞について，自動詞ならば I，他動詞ならば T を書きなさい．

1) Yesterday I got up at six, and had breakfast at seven. [　]
2) I know that Korean movie star very well. [　]
3) Today's newspaper says that the president will retire next March. [　]
4) We were sitting on a bench until the next train arrived. [　]
5) Thomas entered the front door during the lecture. [　]
6) Please come to our new house if you visit this town. [　]

2. 次の 1)～4) の a. b. の下線部の対は同形の動詞の自動詞 (a.)／他動詞 (b.) です．それぞれ日本語に訳しなさい．

1) a. Robert stopped to tie his shoes.
   b. Robert stopped the taxi and went to the hotel.
2) a. We shouldn't speak ill of others.
   b. When Japanese people speak English, they often make phonetic mistakes.
3) a. Emily always writes to Jennifer by snail mail, not by e-mail.
   b. Last year Emily wrote five academic papers.
4) a. I believed in Santa Claus until I was 10 years old.
   b. I believe you even if most of our classmates said you told a lie.

3. 次の 1）〜 3）の日本文の下線部の動詞が英語では自動詞（（ ）の動詞）で表現されることを考慮して，全体を英語に訳しなさい．
1) 新幹線は，17：10 に東京駅に到着した (arrive)．
2) このナイフは本当によく切れる (cut)．
3) 地球上の空気は，主に窒素と酸素で成り立っている (consist)．

（窒素：nitrogen, 酸素：oxygen）

4. 次の 1）〜 3）の日本文の下線部の動詞が英語では他動詞（（ ）の動詞）で表現されることを考慮して，全体を英語に訳しなさい．
1) そのパン屋は，1 日に 100 個のパンを焼く (bake)．

（パン 1 個：a loaf of bread）

2) 先月さおりは鳥取砂丘を初めて訪れた (visit)．

（鳥取砂丘：Tottori Sand Dune）

3) うちの隣の家は，ペットの猫を 3 匹飼っている (have)．

覚えておきたい英単語　　**2 町の施設など**

駅	station
郵便局	post office
ホテル	hotel
警察署	police station
裁判所	court of law
市役所	city hall
県庁	prefectural office
税務署	tax office
デパート	department store
モール	shopping mall

| 第**3**章 | 主語と述語（動詞） |

文の構造

文（**sentence**）とは，英語の場合，アルファベットの大文字で書き始めて**ピリオド**（**period** " . "），**疑問符**（**question mark** " ? "），**感嘆符**（**exclamation mark** " ! "）で終わる一連のものであるが，"Oh!" "Wow!" などの叫び声や "Yes." "No." などの応答（返事）の場合を除いて，ある一貫した構造をもっている．それは，述べられた内容の主体を表す**主語**（**subject**）とそれの作用や動作を表す**述語**（**predicate**）をかならずもっていることである．英語の場合は述語は必ず**動詞**（**verb**）であり，**述語動詞**（**predicate verb**）といわれる．あらゆる文には主語と述語動詞（以下単に「動詞」と言及する）が必ず 1 つずつあり，平叙文の場合は，

主語（S）― 動詞（V）

の順序にならぶ．これを仮に「SV 構造」と呼ぶ．

5 文型といわれているものも，所詮はすべて SV 構造をもっている．

第 1 文型（**SV**）：　The plane flew in the air.
　　　　　　　　　　　S　　V

第 2 文型（**SVC**）：　Betty got angry.
　　　　　　　　　　　S　　V　C

第 3 文型（**SVO**）：　Korean people usually eat kimchi.
　　　　　　　　　　　S　　　　　　　V　O

第 4 文型（**SVOO**）：　I gave her a present for her birthday.
　　　　　　　　　　　S　V　O　　O

第 5 文型（**SVOC**）：　Takeshi named his dog John.
　　　　　　　　　　　S　　V　　O　　C

疑問文

SV 構造をもつ文が**疑問文**（**yes-no 疑問文**）になる時，語順に関しては次の 2 つのパターンがある．

1) be 動詞，have＋過去分詞（完了相），助動詞＋動詞原形の場合

☞ be あるいは have，助動詞と主語の位置が入れ替わる．

He is a teacher. → Is he a teacher?
S V   V S

I must pay ¥1,000 for the entrance fee.
S V

→ Must I pay ¥1,000 for the entrance fee?
         V S

2) 一般動詞の場合

☞ do を助動詞として使い，元の動詞は原形になる．この場合，do は主語や時制に応じて活用する（例えば，三人称単数現在形の場合，do は does になる）．do は主語 S の前にくる．

John walks to school every day. → Does John walk to school every day?
S V   S
                               V

否定文

否定文は，not をそえるが，その作り方は疑問文の 2 つの基準にしたがう．

1) be 動詞，have＋過去分詞（完了相），助動詞＋動詞原形の場合

☞ be, have, 助動詞のあとに not を添える．

We can't (＜ cannot※) cross the street when the traffic light is red.

※通常 "can not" のように離して書かない．

2) 一般動詞の場合

☞ 疑問文の場合と同様，do を用い，do not (＞ don't) ＋動詞原形とする．do は主語や時制に応じて活用する．

I didn't (＜ did not) have any books on philosophy in my office.

否定疑問文

yes-no 疑問文が否定の形になっているものを否定疑問文というが，この場合，応答の "yes/no" は日本語の「はい／いいえ」ではなく，「いいえ／はい」に対応する．英語の場合，質問文が肯定／否定のいずれであっても，答えが肯定な

15

らば yes，否定ならば no がそれぞれ対応するが，日本語では，質問文の叙述内容に忠実な応答が「はい」で，叙述内容に反する場合が「いいえ」になる．つまり否定疑問文の場合，質問文の叙述に反する肯定となる応答は，英語で "yes," 日本語で「いいえ」，質問文の叙述に忠実な否定の応答は，英語で "no," 日本語で「はい」というように，肯定疑問文の場合とは逆の対応をすることになる．

Don't you know that famous TV star? — Unfortunately, no. I rarely watch TV.
「あの有名なテレビのスター，知らないの？」―「残念ながらそのとおり．僕はあんまりテレビ見ないもので.」

Exercise 3

1. 次の各文の SV 構造を，例に従って示しなさい．

例：<u>The jet plane</u> <u>flew</u> in the air.
        S   V

1) People living in rural areas hardly know the difficulty of riding on the overcrowded trains.
2) To tell the truth, I didn't go to that place.
3) Yesterday we had heavy snow in this town.
4) It is cloudy today.
5) As for me, I cannot visit your house by car because I don't have a driver's license.
6) According to the weather forecast it will be colder tomorrow.
7) Despite his age he doesn't have any health problems.
8) Walking along the beach I found a nice shaped shell in the sand.

2. 次の英文を yes-no 疑問文にしなさい．

1) You are a staff member of this company.
2) There are some questions about this lecture.
3) Masahiko can speak Chinese at a normal speed.
4) You went to Okayama by train last month.
5) He collects rare old coins.
6) He has ever been to Korea before.

3. 次の英文を否定文にしなさい.

1) This is my telephone number.

2) I'm American.

3) He made a list of items they ordered yesterday.

4) Michael might go to such a dangerous place alone.

5) You have an agenda of the last meeting.

6) You have seen the famous movie.

4. 次の英文をそれぞれ日本語に訳しなさい.

1) Don't you think that smoking in public is rather impolite? — Yes, of course, but I like smoking.

2) Don't you see my wristwatch that I left on my desk a little earlier? — No. I don't see it.

3) Aren't you our client calling about a legal case? — Yes. It's me!

覚えておきたい
英単語 　**3** 交通・通学（通勤）

飛行機	aircraft
新幹線	Shinkansen / bullet train
連絡船	ferry line
バス停	bus stop
バスターミナル	bus terminal
出発	departure
到着	arrival
乗り物で通学する（通勤する）	commute
Ａ線に乗り換える	transfer to the A Line
切符売り場	ticket counter
落とし物預かり所	lost and found office
定期乗車券	commuter pass
運賃	fare

17

| 第**4**章 | 動詞の時制（1）・進行相・完了相 |

英語の時制と時間指示

英語の時制は，**現在時制**（**present tense**），**過去時制**（**past tense**），**未来時制**（**future tense**）の 3 つがある．名称から推測されるのは，それぞれ，「現在」「過去」「未来」の指示に関わることであるが，実際にはかなり異なる．名前通りの指示をするのは過去時制ぐらいである．

現在時制と現在

「現在時制は，現在を指示する」といえば，さも当然のように感じられるが，そうでない場合が多い．現在の動作を表す場合は，通常，**現在進行形**（**present progressive**）が使われる．進行形でない現在形は，習慣的な動作を表す．

I'm reading a newspaper now.（現在の動作）

I walk for an hour for my health every day.（習慣的な動作）

"be going to ～" の形は，be が現在形でも未来のことを表現している．

We are going to climb Mt. Daisen next summer.

確定的な未来を現在形で表すこともできる．

According to the schedule, I leave this town the day after tomorrow.

未来時制

未来時制は "will＋動詞原形" で表現される．

We will hold the annual conference for this year next March.

この文の時間指示は「未来」であるが，推量，意志の助動詞 will としての解釈も可能である．「未来」の表現は，実際に起こっていない出来事に関するものであるから，想像の域を出ないからであろう．

For the next examination, I will do my best.

As the lock is very old, the door won't open easily.

18

進行相と完了相

話し手が，できごとをどのような視点で考えているかを表す動詞の側面を**相**（**aspect**）という．英語で体系的に相を表現しているのは進行相と完了相である．

進行相

進行中の動作を表す動詞の相を**進行相**（**progressive**）という．進行相は「進行形」として言及される．進行形には「現在進行形」「過去進行形」「未来進行形」という3つの時制がある．時間指示はそれぞれほぼ「現在」「過去」「未来」である．進行相で表現できるのは動作動詞のみである．「現在進行形」は「現在」という時間の動作を表すにはもっとも典型的な動詞形であるといえる．形は**"be＋〜ing（現在分詞）"**であり，"be"の時制によって「現在進行形」「過去進行形」「未来進行形」になる．

Children are reading picture books in the nursery.

Paul was watching TV when his mother came home.

We'll be playing tennis at this time tomorrow.

*I am having a dog in my house.（"have"は状態動詞，*は成り立たない文を表す．）

過去進行形だけは，「〜することろだった／〜しかけた」の意味を持つことがある．

While I was leaving home, the telephone rang.

完了相

動作が完結し，その叙述内容が後の時点になんらかの関わりをもっていることを表す動詞の相は**完了相**（**perfective**）と呼ばれる．初等文法では「完了」「継続」「経験」の3つの意味に分類されるが，これらは共通して過去の叙述内容が時間的により後の時点になんらかの関わりをもつ，ということにおいては共通している．形は**"have＋過去分詞"**である．この場合"have"は「もつ」という一般の動詞ではなく，完了相に関わる助動詞であるという解釈から，疑問，否定は，"can""must"など，"助動詞＋動詞原形"の形の助動詞の場合と同じにふるまう．

19

[肯定] I have forgotten our promise.

[疑問] Have you been to America in the last five years?

[否定] She hasn't seen his lost wallet.

[完了の意味] …… 動作が完了し，終わったことが後の時点に関わる場合

　　Have you finished your homework yet?

[継続の意味] …… 動作／状態がそのまま継続している場合

　　Susie has lived in Morioka since she got married.

[経験の意味] …… 以前の動作／状態を後の時点から振り返っている場合

　　Jack was always saying that he had seen an alien in his elementary school.

過去完了

　過去完了だけは，表現すべき時間差のある過去の表現のうち，より古い方の過去の時間指示をするのに使われる．この過去完了は，時制の一致が関係した場合にも使われる．これは前ページの「完了」「継続」「経験」の3分類とは関係がない．

　When we arrived at Tottori Station, the express train bound for Kyoto had left the platform.

Exercise 4

1. 次の各文の（ ）の動詞を過去形に直し，全文を日本語に訳しなさい．

1) Yesterday morning there (be) a fire in the town.

2) At the beginning of the conference the chair person (announce) the agenda.

3) Last week I accidentally (meet) Professor Kato in the department store.

4) When I was young, I (visit) the Great Pyramid in Egypt.

2. 次の各文は，「（単純形の）現在形」と「現在進行形」のどちらを使うべきか．それぞれ考えてどちらかの形にしなさい．

1) Two plus three (equal) five.

2) Tom (play) tennis at the tennis court now.

3) Watch out! A little boy (cross) the crosswalk now!

4) Mr. Watanabe (have) a crocodile as a pet. It's dangerous.

3. 次の各文の動詞部分（下線部）を（ ）の完了相にし，全体を書きかえなさい．

1) Do you submit a term report yet?（現在完了）

2) James gets the degree of Ph.D. in linguistics by next February.（未来完了）

3) Kaori sees the aurora in the sky in Finland.（現在完了）

4) When I came home, I found that I left my briefcase at my office.（過去完了）

覚えておきたい
英単語

4 観光・出張・旅行

観光	sightseeing
出張	business trip
旅行会社	travel agency
旅程表	itinerary
予約	reservation
搭乗口	boarding gate
搭乗手続き	boarding procedure
懇親会	banquet
格安チケット	discounted ticket
払い戻し	refund

21

第**5**章　　進行相

進行相とは

進行相（**progressive**）とは，動作がある時点で進行している様態を表し，基本的には"be 〜 ing"で示され，(1) 現在進行形「〜している」，(2) 過去進行形「〜していた」，(3) 未来進行形「(未来のある時点で) 〜しているだろう」にそれぞれ分類できる.

　時間軸上で時点として表される**時制**（**tense**）とは異なり，**相**（**aspect**）は，時間軸上にある時点を輪切りにして考えるとよい.

進行相の分類

　先に述べた進行相を，各時制の単純形と比較して，時間軸上でイメージしてみよう（※未来進行形については，現在進行形と比較する）．なお，ここでいう時点は，過去，現在，未来を時間軸上の点で示したものである.

(1)　現在進行形　be（現在形）〜 ing: 〜している

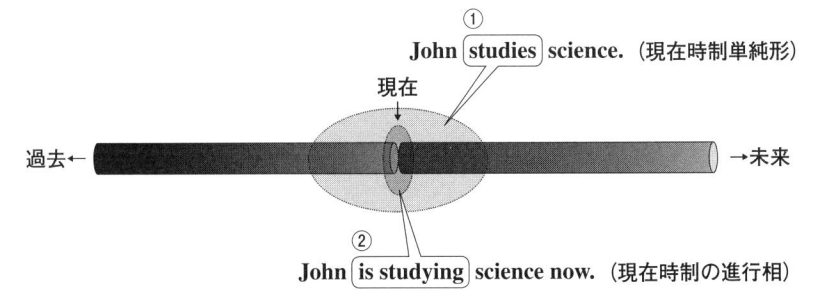

　①，②ともに話者がイメージする時点は，「現在」という点で一致している.しかしながら，同じ「現在」でも，①は時間軸上の時点を指し，②は時間軸上の時点を輪切りにした**切り口全体**を指し，その中で動作が進行していることを示す.

（2）　過去進行形　be（過去形）〜 ing: 〜していた

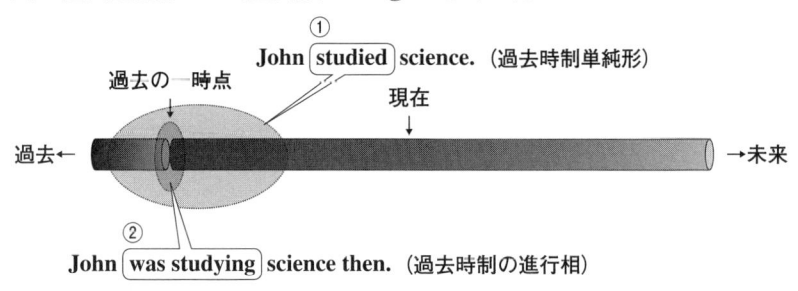

　①, ②ともに話者が言及する時点は,「過去」という点で一致している. また, 時間軸上の解釈は, 現在進行形のケースをそのまま過去に移動させるというイメージで捉えるとよい.

（3）　未来進行形　will be 〜 ing: 〜しているだろう

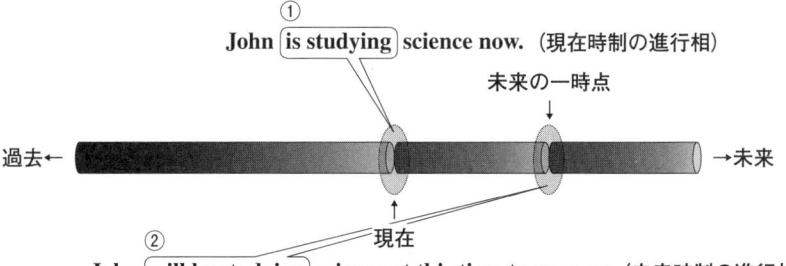

　①, ②ともに話者がイメージする時点は, 時間軸上の時点で完全に異なる. ①は時間軸上の現在, ②は時間軸上の未来の時点を輪切りにした**切り口全体**を指し, それぞれの層の中で動作が進行していることを示す.

その他の用法

　上に示した進行相は, 基本的には「時点」として表されるものであった. それ以外にも, （4）動作が一定範囲行われているもの, （5）副詞（always, constantly など）を伴うことで, 動作が繰り返し行われているもの, （6）進行相と受動態（passive voice）との組み合わせ, （7）近未来を示すものがある.

(4) 動作が一定範囲行われている.
Nancy was practicing her guitar all the afternoon.

(5) 動作が繰り返し行われている.
Tom is always complaining about my opinions. (頻度を表す副詞と併用)

(6) 進行相と受動態との組み合わせ "be being 過去分詞"「～されている」
A new city hall is being built over there.

(7) 近未来 (近い未来の予定を示し, 具体的な準備が整えられている状況)
He is making a presentation tomorrow. Everyone is looking forward to it.

Exercise 5

1. 1) ～ 5) のうち, 英文として成立するものには○を, 不成立のものには×
と表記しなさい. ×のものについては, 正しい形に直しなさい.
1) My sister is resembling her grandmother.
2) Jane was studying Japanese history when I visited her last night.
3) They are having lunch at the school cafeteria.
4) After graduating from college, Tom will be working for the company.
5) We are knowing that water boils at 100℃.

2. 進行形の用法を答え, 全文を日本語に訳しなさい. なお, 進行形の用法に
ついては, 以下の選択肢から選ぶこと.
1) When I got home, the wall was being painted by my father.
2) They were talking about the important matter all night long.
3) Everyone is constantly complaining about the way he behaves.
4) I'm leaving Japan for China tomorrow, so I have to pack my clothes in
the bag.
　　選択肢： a.「動作の繰り返し」 b.「進行相と受動態との組み合わせ」
　　　　　　 c.「近未来」　　　　　 d.「一定範囲行われる動作」

24

3. 与えられた日本語の意味に合うように，[ ] 内の語(句)を並べ替えなさい. ただし，文頭は大文字で始めること.

1) 彼は，来月の終わりには新宿支店で勤務しているだろう.

He [for / the end / branch office / be / of / working / at / the Shinjuku / will] next month.

2) その高価な車は，指定された場所に停めようとしていた.

[stopping / area / car / the expensive / at / was / the designated].

4. それぞれの日本文の全文を英語に訳しなさい.

1) だんだん寒くなっている. 温かい飲み物を買いに行こう.

2) 彼が教室に入った時，クラスの皆が試験に向けて勉強をしていた.

3) 多くの乗客達が，その事故で瀕死の状態になった.

4) あなたは今晩 7 時に彼女とおしゃべりをしていると思いました.

覚えておきたい英単語 **⑤ 行政・市民生活**

住民票	certificate of residence
確定申告	final income tax return
水道の供給	water service
電気料金	electric bill
選挙	election
投票	voting
市長	mayor
市議会・町議会	assembly
選挙区	constituency
（自治体・国家の）予算	budget
決算	settlement of accounts
基幹施設（インフラ）	infrastructure
道路整備	road improvement
下水道設備	drainage / sewer

| 第**6**章 | 完了相 |

完了相とは

　完了相（**perfective**）は，動作がある時点で完了している様態を表す．“(1) have (has) / (2) had / (3) will have ＋[**過去分詞**]” の形で示され，それぞれ (1) 現在完了形，(2) 過去完了形，(3) 未来完了形として分類できる．時間軸上で完了形をイメージする場合，発話時点での**時間指示**（**time reference**）と，言及する動作や状態が始まった時間指示とを結び付けて考えるとよい．

完了相の分類

　第5章の進行形と同様，完了形を時間軸上でイメージしてみよう．ここでは，現在，過去，未来の時間指示と完了形として表現される動作や状態との比較を時間軸上の点で示す．

(1)　現在完了形：（ずっと）～している

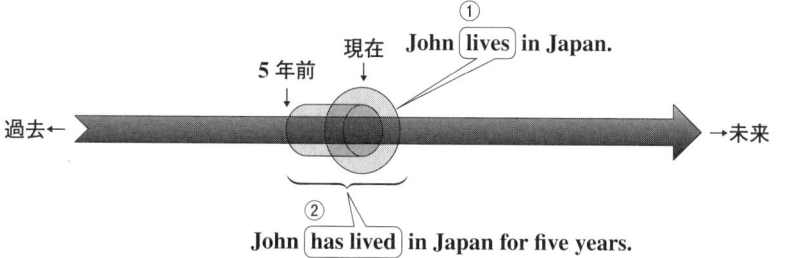

　① で話者が言及する時点は，「現在」のみである．一方 ② では，時間軸上の5年前の時点と現在の時点を結び付け，その間「（ずっと）日本に住んでいる」という状態が継続していることを示す．

　完了形には，継続，完了，経験の3用法があるが，それぞれの用法を区別するための判断材料（キーワード）を以下の表に示す．

用法	判断材料（キーワード）
継続	for ～（～の間），since ～（～以来，～から）
完了	just（ちょうど），already（もう，すでに），yet（まだ，もう）
経験	ever（これまでに），never（一度も～ない），before（以前），～ times（～回），etc.

(2)　過去完了形：〜してしまった

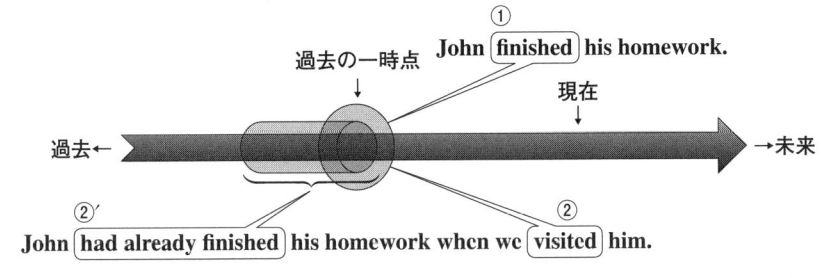

　①, ② で話者がイメージする時点は，「過去の任意の時点」のみであり，現在との結び付きはない．一方，②′ は，② との関連において，それより過去の時点の出来事であることを示す必要がある．このような場合に過去完了形が用いられることになる．②′ は，①,② と同様に，現在の時点との結び付きはないと捉える．

(3)　未来完了形：〜してしまっているだろう

John $\boxed{\text{will finish}}$ his essay next month.
来月
John $\boxed{\text{will have finished}}$ his essay by the next month.

① で話者がイメージする時点は，「来月」という漠然とした未来の任意の時点のみであり，その時点での動作を推測している．一方，② では，時間軸上の「来月」という未来の時点に言及し，「その時点までにエッセイを書き終えてしまっているだろう」という動作の**完了**を示す．つまり，任意の未来の時点とそれより前の時点（通常未来の一時点）とを結び付けている．

┃その他の用法

　上に示した完了形以外に，**現在／過去／未来完了進行形**があり，"have (has) been/had been/will have been 〜ing" の形で示される．ここでは，現在完了進行形を例に，時間軸上での解釈を説明する．

27

(4) 現在完了進行形：（ずっと）～し続けている

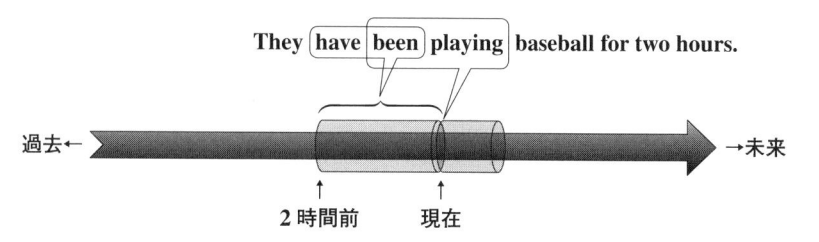

They [have [been] playing] baseball for two hours.

過去← →未来

2 時間前　　現在

　話者が言及している時点は，「野球をし始めた 2 時間前」からこの話をしている「現在」までであり，これは完了形の "have been" の部分で表現されている．さらに，進行形は現在の時点を輪切りにした切り口全体を示し（上の図を参照），それは "been playing" の部分で示されることになる．この解釈は「野球をする」という動作が 2 時間ずっと続いていて，今も進行中ということを含意している．また，過去／未来完了進行形においても，この図式を用いて同様の解釈が得られる．

Exercise 6

1. 下線部の完了形の用法を「継続，完了，経験」から選び，全文を日本語に訳しなさい．

1) They <u>will have been</u> married for 15 years next month.

2) I <u>had</u> never <u>owned</u> my own computer before I entered college.

3) Due to the bad wheather, the construction <u>hasn't finished</u> yet.

2. 1)～4) のうち，英文として成立するものには○を，不成立のものには×と表記しなさい．×のものについては，正しい形に直しなさい．

1) When have you finished your report on environmental pollution?

2) How long have you been waiting for her at the bus stop?

3) John had already left for France when she called him two hours before.

4) He was repairing his motorcycle for three hours before we visited him.

28

3. それぞれの日本文の全文を英語に訳しなさい.

1) 私は今月で，この部署 (department) での任務が終了します.

2) 「お久ぶりですね.」「元気でしたか？」

3) 台風が町を直撃する前に，彼らは避難を完了した.

4) 先月失くした運転免許証 (driver's license) を昨日見つけた.

覚えておきたい
英単語

6 福祉・保険

福祉	welfare
社会保障	social security
介護保険	nursing care insurance
介護士	care worker
老人介護	care for the aged
託児所	nursery
民生委員	caseworker
育児休暇	child-care leave
フレックスタイム制	flexible working hours
年金	pension
公的年金制度	public pension plan
高齢化社会	aging society
寝たきり老人	bedridden elderly people
デイサービスセンター	day service center

第**7**章　名詞と冠詞

可算名詞と不可算名詞

可算名詞（**countable noun**）：単数形・複数形の区別をする.

friend, scientist; apple, potato; city, country
family, class, audience, team, police

We made a lot of **friends** in the first year of university.
There are 300 **families** living in the settlement.
The **family** are looking for someone who speaks English.
　（集合的に複数として扱う単数形）
Little good **news** are also good news.
The good **news** is that it's not hard to become a better dancer.
　（形は複数形だが単数の扱い）
He bought three pairs of **shoes** for £20 each.（一対を表す複数形）

不可算名詞（**uncountable noun**）：原則として複数形で用いない.

air, bread, gold, rice, water
freedom, furniture, information, knowledge, music
George, London, Moonlight Sonata, Aeneid, Audi

You will learn how to make delicious **bread**.
Whenever you drink some **water**, think about the source of it.
The museum has been collecting **furniture** and **woodwork** for over 150 years.
Please do not bring large **luggage**, suitcases, cabin bags and other oversized objects to the museum.
Beethoven lived during one of the most unstable periods in European history.

用法により可算・不可算どちらにもなりうる名詞にも注意が必要である.

30

Coffee is offered when visiting friends, during festivities, or as a daily element of life.

We offer a full bar service with bottled **beers**, house and finest **wines**, soft **drinks**, freshly brewed **tea**, a selection of **coffees** and hot **chocolate**.

If you are having **difficulty** with your course, want to talk about your condition or need advice, please get in touch with us.

Some people with learning **disabilities** may have additional **difficulties** such as physical or sensory impairment.

■ 不定冠詞と定冠詞, 無冠詞

(1) 不定冠詞 (indefinite article)：a/an

主に可算名詞の単数形とともに用いられる.「1」を表すはたらきが基本である. 不特定・一般のものを表す機能から様々な用法が派生している.

There was **a** car which left Sendai at **an** early hour.

How many pianos can **a** piano tuner tune in **a** year?

Our library was given **a** sizable collection of Roman antiquities by **a** Mrs. Morrow.

(2) 定冠詞 (definite article)：the

「その」という指示のはたらきが基本であるが, 特定・唯一のものを表すことで, 不定冠詞と対比される.

I bought a cellphone. **The** camera of **the** phone was very good.

The only person that should know your password is YOU.

Help yourself to **the** complimentary tea and coffee.

(3) 無冠詞 (zero article)：ø (冠詞を用いない)

名詞が本来の機能を果たすことを表す場合や, 身分を表す名詞が文中で補語として用いられる場合などの他, 複数名詞が不定であることも示す.

Studying at ø university is very different from ø high school or ø junior high.

I was appointed ø supervisor in Chemistry at Trinity College.

ø Doctors quite rightly say that eating ø apples is good for one's health.

31

可算名詞の単数形・複数形と定・不定

　冠詞と単数形・複数形の組み合わせにより，名詞は初めて十全な意味機能を持つ．可算名詞に関して以下の図式で理解しておくと，実用上便利である．

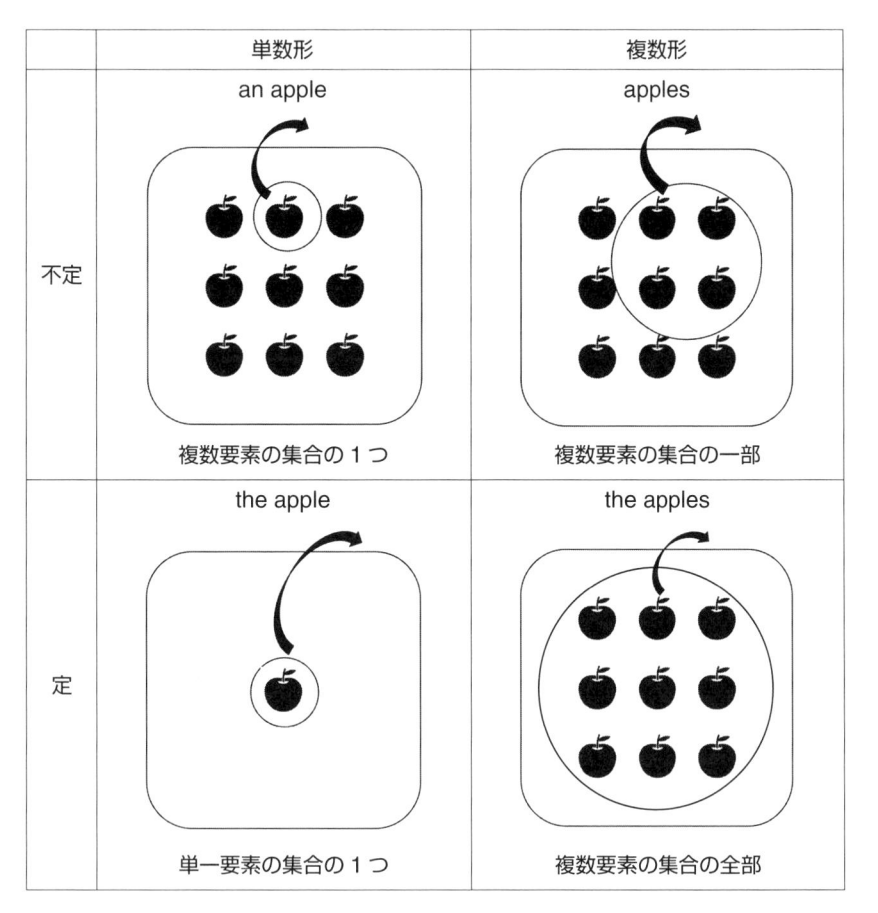

Exercise 7

1. 日本語に訳しなさい．

1) After the Romans arrived, a large-scale pottery industry developed in Britain.

2) Improvements in medical technology made a major contribution to the reduction in fatality rate during the period.

3) The collections in the Louvre make up a significant part of the standard of Western European art.

4) Even though it was quite an unusual approach in psychology, the teachers were very supportive in helping to carry out my plan.

2. 英語に訳しなさい.

1) 私の家族はみんな元気で，また君に会えるのを楽しみにしている.

2) 彼女はパン，牛乳，バターを買いに，自分の娘をその店に行かせた.

3) 一通の電子メールが友人から私に転送されてきたのは，ある月曜日の朝9時のことだった.（転送される：be forwarded to）

覚えておきたい英単語 　７ 政治

上院／参議院	the House of Councilors / the Upper House
下院／衆議院	the House of Representatives / the Lower House
国会	Diet (日本) / Parliament (英国) / Congress (米国)
内閣	cabinet
（総理）大臣	(Prime) Minister
政党	political party
与党	ruling party
野党	opposition party
民主主義	democracy
共産主義	communism
共和国	republic
官僚／官僚主義	bureaucracy

第8章 代名詞

代名詞の種類

(1) **人称代名詞**（**personal pronoun**）：人称（一人称・二人称・三人称）と
数（単数・複数）の区別をする：I, you, he / she / it; we, you, they
格変化（主格・所有格・目的格）をする．また所有代名詞・再帰代名詞
の形を持つ：I – my – me – mine – myself など．

(2) **指示代名詞**（**demonstrative pronoun**）：this, these; that, those

(3) **不定代名詞**（**indefinite pronoun**）：one; another, other; some, any; all,
none; each, every; somebody, something; both, either, neither

(4) **疑問代名詞**（**interrogative pronoun**）：who – whose – whom, which, what

(5) **関係代名詞**（**relative pronoun**）：who – whose – whom, which, that, what

人称代名詞の用法

人称代名詞は，英語では主格，所有格，目的格を区別する．主格は文中で主
語や主格補語になり，所有格は所有関係を表し，目的格は動詞や前置詞の目的
語になる．

She often wrote letters to her children.（主格）

My current research is about the relation between language and society.（所有格）

They never showed any bad feelings toward us .（目的格）

所有代名詞（**possessive pronoun**）は「所有格＋名詞」のはたらきをし，「〜
のもの」という意味になる．

This report is hers . Where is mine ?（＝ her report; my report）

再帰代名詞（**reflexive pronoun**）は主語の動作が自分に向けられること（再
帰）を表し，「〜自身」という意味になる．また，名詞・代名詞を強める（強調）
はたらきを持つ．

再帰：He seems to think of himself as a Japanese.

強調：I started the Vegetarian Society six months after I myself became a vegetarian.

指示代名詞の用法

指示代名詞 this, these は話者から見て位置的・心理的に近いもの，that, those は遠いものを示すのが基本である．

This is my chair and that is yours.

不定代名詞の用法

不特定の人やものを示すのが基本であるが，それぞれについて用法を学ぶ必要がある．

One can download the software for free.

Each of the approaches has advantages and disadvantages.

Both of the children were born in Italy.

疑問代名詞の用法

人やものごとに関する疑問を表し，疑問文を作るはたらきを持つ．

Whose calculator shows the nearest number to 19?

Which flavor do you like the most?

What made you behave in that way?

代名詞 it の用法

① it ~ that … や it ~ to … の形で，文中で形式主語・形式目的語（仮主語・仮目的語）としてはたらく．

It is important that we act quickly to stop this malware.

Most students found it quite difficult to understand the mechanism.

② 天候・時間・距離などを表す it を，**非人称** (**impersonal**) の it と呼ぶ．

It is going to snow tomorrow.

What time is it now?

It was a long journey to Seattle.

Exercise 8

1. 人称代名詞の主格・所有格・目的格・所有代名詞形・再帰代名詞形を書きなさい．

I – my – me – mine – myself

you（単数）

he

she

it

we

you（複数）

they

2. 日本語に訳しなさい．

1) This picture of yours is extraordinary.

2) The field of research will be determined by the students themselves.

3) There is something wrong with your OS installation.

4) It is not good for your health to skip breakfast.

3. 英語に訳しなさい．

1) ホテルから私たちのキャンパスまでは歩いてすぐです．（a short walk）

2) それがあなたの最終的な答えですか．

3) 私たち自身の結果と彼らの結果を比較しなさい．

覚えておきたい
英単語

8 病院・病気・症状

診療所・個人病院	clinic
診察	medical check-up
診察券	patient's registration card
診断	diagnosis
血圧	blood pressure
高血圧	high blood pressure
花粉症	hay fever / pollinosis
拒食症	anorexia
癌	cancer
糖尿病	diabetes
肺炎	pneumonia
認知症	dementia
不眠症	insomnia
食中毒	food poisoning
処方箋	prescription
虫刺され	insect bite
高所恐怖症	acrophobia
閉所恐怖症	claustrophobia
対人恐怖症	anthropophobia

第9章　前置詞

前置詞の用法

前置詞（**preposition**）は名詞・代名詞や名詞相当語句と結びついて**前置詞句**（**prepositional phrase**）を形成し，文中で形容詞や副詞のはたらきをする．第15章「句と節」では，句の分類は，文中での働きに従う分類をしており，前置詞句という分類はおこなってない．ここでいう「前置詞句」はその働きにしたがって，形容詞句と副詞句として扱っている（p. 62 以降参照）．

The book on the desk is written in Latin.

（形容詞のはたらき＝第15章の「形容詞句」）

Children were playing with toys.　　（副詞のはたらき＝第15章の「副詞句」）

前置詞の位置

名詞・代名詞や名詞相当語句を目的語として取り，その直前に置かれるのが原則である．

Many students had difficulty in writing reports.　　（前置詞＋動名詞）

Please talk about why you wish to learn about film.　　（前置詞＋名詞節）

疑問詞や関係代名詞を目的語として取る場合などは，それらの語が前に移動するので，互いに遊離する．

What are you talking about?　　　　　　　　（about と what が遊離）

The laboratory (which / that) his father works in is located in the building.

（in と which/that が遊離）

前置詞の分類

前置詞は場所・時・方向・原因・理由・手段などを表すが，それぞれの前置詞の基本的な意味をとらえ，そこから派生するさまざまなはたらきを関連づけて理解することが重要である．

(1) 場所：about, above, among, around／round, at, behind, beside, between, in, on, over, near など.

Train tickets can be purchased at the station's ticket office.
The town is 250m above sea level.
It is nice to be outside, to be among the trees and feel the fresh air.
The stage is set up near the lake and is surrounded by different food and drink vendors.
In the photograph Professor Morrow is standing between Dr. Kato and Dr. Tanaka.

(2) 時：after, at, before, by, during, for, from, in, on, since, through, to, until／till, within など.

We are working from nine in the morning until six in the evening.
You can translate this paper within an hour.
We could easily make the 8km hike to the castle and get back before dark.
The next meeting will be held on Wednesday, 22 April 2018 at 4:00 p.m. in the meeting room, Level 2, Queen Mary University.
Since 2005 she has been collaborating in research projects with the Philosophy Research Center of the University of Tokyo.

(3) 方向：across, along, for, into, through, to, toward／towards など.

I often get into trouble because I don't think before acting.
There is a safe way to exit the room through the window.
This is a bad time to take a walk along the beach.
Everyone is invited to join us for lunch at the restaurant across the street once the seminar concludes.
Two policemen were moving with great speed towards the gate.

(4) 原因・理由：at, from, of, through, with など.

We are delighted at the news of his Nobel Prize Award.
By the end of the day I am very tired from all those things to do.
Health policies are failed through a fundamental lack of clinical

39

understanding or consultation.

Students are absent from school with a variety of health problems.

One third of us will die of cancer.

(5)　手段：by, in, on, with など．

The fare between Paris and London by airplane is not much more than by rail.

The documents were written with a typewriter.

He began composing and performing on the piano from an early age with the help of his mother.

Everyone learns in their own way.

句前置詞

　2語以上からなり，前置詞と同様のはたらきを持つものを**句前置詞**または**群前置詞**（**phrasal preposition**）と呼ぶ：according to, as for, as to, because of, by means of, by way of, in addition to, in case of, in spite of, instead of, on account of, owing to, thanks to など．

due to 〜：〜のため
　The flight was cancelled due to the bad weather.

as of 〜：〜現在
　As of March 2017, there were 1,853 applications to the scholarship.

on behalf of 〜：〜に代わって，〜を代表して
　On behalf of our college, I welcome you to the new academic year.

Exercise 9

1.　次の各文の（　）内に適切な前置詞を入れなさい．

1) John and Ann heard someone crying (　　) help.

2) The images are displayed (　　) the whiteboard by a digital projector.

3) Contestants will try to eat as many hamburgers as possible (　　) ten minutes.

4) Alcohol consumption (　　) young people in Japan appears to have fallen in recent years.

5) The poet produced about 100 works, many of them were translated ( ) English.

2. 日本語に訳しなさい.
1) The government provided free medical treatment for refugees from across the border.
2) These books are written in terms of what the reader wants to know.
3) It was with surprise that we discovered bacteria in a lake beneath Antarctica.
4) Students were asked to stand in a line in the hallway.

3. 英語に訳しなさい.
1) 私はこのイベントのために充分なお金を稼ぐという仕事を与えられた.
2) この ID カードを使えば，お金を持っていなくても安全に帰宅することができる.
3) スタジオの閉じたドアの後ろから音楽が聞こえてきた.（後ろから：from behind）

覚えておきたい英単語

❾ 不動産・賃貸契約

不動産	real estate
地所・不動産物件	estate
賃貸マンション	rental apartment / apartment on lease
賃貸料	rent
契約	contract
敷金・頭金	deposit
礼金	reward
引っ越し業者	moving company
火災保険	fire insurance
災害保険	casualty insurance
損害保険	damage insurance
10 階建てのマンション	ten-story apartment building

第10章　形容詞と副詞

形容詞と副詞のはたらき

　文は動詞を中心として作られる．主語や目的語など，それぞれの動詞が必要とする要素がそろうことで文は出来上がる．次の文は，動詞 "sang (< sing)" を文の中心とする他動詞文である．

（1）　The boy sang a song.

　（1）は，動詞 "sang" と2つの名詞 "the boy" と "a song" からなる文で，「少年が歌を歌った」という事実を簡潔に述べている文である．しかしながら，これらの動詞や名詞だけで描くことのできる状況には語彙的な制限があるために，この文からは，例えば「少年の特徴や様子」あるいは「少年がどんな歌をどのように歌ったのか」などについての情報は得られない．（1）に修飾語句である形容詞や副詞を添えることで，より詳しい状況などを述べることができる．

（2）　The little boy sang a traditonal song very well.

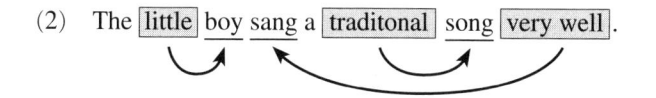

　（2）では，主語 "boy" と目的語 "song" の名詞の前にそれぞれ形容詞 "little" と "traditional" が，また，文末には副詞 "very well" が置かれている．形容詞は後続する名詞を，また，文末の副詞は動詞 "sang" を修飾している．いわゆる「修飾−被修飾」という関係は，例えば（2）であれば，修飾語句である形容詞 "little" と "traditional" および副詞 "very well" が被修飾語句である名詞や動詞に情報を付け加えるということである．このように形容詞と副詞は動詞と名詞だけでは描ききれない出来事の詳細について叙述することを可能にし，言語表現を豊かなものにしてくれる．

形容詞の2つの用法

　形容詞は主語や目的語に現れる名詞を直接修飾するだけではなく，動詞の補語として文内で独立した要素としても機能する．

(3)　There was a broken camera on the desk.

(4)　The camera on the desk was broken.
　　　　　　　　　　　　　　　　　V　C

(5)　I took the camera out of the bag only to found it broken.
　　　　　　　　　　　　　　　　　　　V　O　C

　(3) では形容詞（過去分詞）"broken" は後続する名詞を直接修飾しており，**限定用法**と呼ばれる．形容詞が単独で使われる場合，形容詞は修飾する名詞の前に置くが，形容詞が他の語句をともなって形容詞句を作る場合，次のように形容詞句は修飾する名詞の後に置かれる．

(6)　They are looking for a person skilled in home nursing.

　(6) では形容詞句 "skilled in home nursing" は修飾する名詞の後に置かれている．この語順は関係節や他の語句を伴う分詞などが名詞の後に置かれることと並行的にとらえることができる．
　また，(4) と (5) では形容詞 "broken" がともに動詞の補語として現れている例で，**叙述用法**と呼ばれる．叙述用法で現れる形容詞は，動詞が自動詞の時は主語の名詞について，また動詞が他動詞の場合には目的語の名詞についてその性質や特徴，状態などを述べる．(4) のような文に現れる自動詞は be 動詞のほかに "become, get, seem, look, grow" などがある．(5) のような文に現れる他動詞は "find" のほかに "make, have, keep, leave" などがある．

副詞の用法

　形容詞が名詞を修飾する一方で，副詞は文内のさまざまな語句を修飾することができ，それに応じて文内で副詞が現れる位置も変わる．

(7)　Ms. Tanaka is an internationally famous architect.

(8)　She solved the question easily.

(9) My son often walks to school.

(10) Unfortunately the heavy snow caused a power outage.

　(7) の "internationally" は後続する形容詞 "famous" を修飾する．(8) の "easily" は出来事がどの様に行われたのかを表し，(9) の "often" は出来事の頻度を表している．(8)，(9) は動詞 "solved" "walks" をそれぞれ修飾している．(10) の "unfortunately" は文全体を修飾し，文で表されている出来事に対する話者の評価が述べられている．

Exercise 10

1. 適切な語句を選び，各文を日本語に訳しなさい．
1) It is [uncertain / uncertainly] if the project will be successful.
2) My mother was a [good / well] swimmer in her school days.
3) It rained hard three days [ago / before].
4) The bus [sudden / suddenly] stopped.
5) James runs [more / much] faster than Ted.
6) My daughter hasn't come home [already / yet].
7) Read this manual [careful / carefully] before you use the machine.
8) He can [hard / hardly] write Chinese characters.
9) I live [close / closely] to the station.
10) She will [probable / probably] win.

2. 語句を並べ替えて英文を完成させなさい．
1) I like [this / shirt / blue].
2) The young man [accept / was / to / reluctant] the job offer.
3) Kevin [overtime / often / works].
4) They [happy / looked / very].
5) Taking a walk [your health / good / is / for].
6) We [be / our project / to / found] impractical.
7) We have [clean / the river / keep / to].

44

8) I have [been / Germany / to / never].

9) The building [high / 150 meters / is].

10) She [work / late / is / for / seldom].

覚えておきたい英単語　**10 自動車**

ハンドル	steering wheel
フロントガラス	windshield
ウィンカー	blinker
アクセルペダル	accelerator
ブレーキペダル	brake pedal
バックミラー	rearview mirror
ルームミラー	windshield rearview mirror
クラクション	horn
ガソリンスタンド	gas station / service station
サービスエリア	rest area
駐車場	parking lot
制限速度	speed limit
修理工	mechanic
オイル交換	motor oil change
オートマ	automatic transmission
マニュアル	manual transmission

第11章 関係詞（1） 関係代名詞

関係節の役割と関係代名詞

関係節（**relative clause**）とは先行詞の名詞を意味的に修飾する節であり，形容詞と同じ役割を果たす．

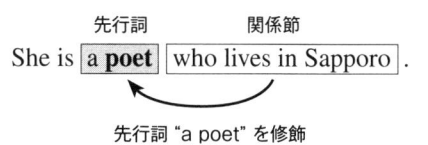

先行詞 "a poet" を修飾

関係節の特徴は，関係詞を取り除くとその後ろの部分に必ず意味的に足りない部分が生じることである．

Tom is a little boy who lives in San Francisco .

☞ 関係詞 "who" を取り除くと，[   ] の節は主格の部分が不足している．(_____ lives in San Francisco)

There are a lot of toys which Jimmy wants to buy .

☞ 関係詞 "which" を取り除くと，[   ] の節は目的格の部分が不足している．(Jimmy wants to buy _____)

Mary has a friend whose mother used to be a jazz singer .

☞ 関係詞 "whose" を取り除くと，[   ] の節は所有格の部分が不足している．(_____ mother used to be a jazz singer)

主格・目的格・所有格の位置の部分が関係詞になったものを**関係代名詞**（**relative pronoun**）といい，関係代名詞となった部分は，意味的に不足する要素となる．

関係代名詞の基本形

先行詞	主格	所有格	目的格
人	who	whose	whom / who
もの	which	whose	which

46

関係代名詞 that

関係代名詞 that が現れるのは，次のような場合が多い．

① 先行詞が疑問詞の who, which の場合
  Who that has a sense of humor can do such a thing?
② 先行詞が，人とものの両方である場合
  I saw Mary and her dog that were about to go for a walk.
③ 先行詞が最上級など，1 人または 1 通りに限定される場合
  He is the tallest man that I have ever met.
④ 関係節の中で意味的に不足する要素が補語の位置の場合
  She is not the smart woman that she used to be.

関係代名詞 what

関係代名詞 what は，先行詞を含む関係代名詞のことで，"the thing which," "something which" などが関係代名詞 what に置き換わる．

  I can't understand the thing which he says.
                        ↓
  I can't understand   what   he says.
  「私は彼の言う**こと**が理解できない．」

関係代名詞 what は，もともとの先行詞の部分 "the thing" を含んでいるため，「もの」「こと」という意味を持ち，英文中に関係詞 what の先行詞は現れない．そのため，関係代名詞 what は文頭でも現れることができる．

  What she said is true.

前置詞＋関係代名詞

関係代名詞が節の初めの位置へ移動するとき，関係代名詞のみではなくそれを含む前置詞句という意味的まとまり**「前置詞＋関係代名詞」全体**で移動する．

47

I read a magazine. + Mr. Watanabe was fully described (in) the magazine .

(in) which

I read a magazine in which Mr. Watanabe was fully described.

上の 2 つの文を，関係詞を使って 1 つの文にすると，"the magazine" が前の文の "a magazine" と同じものを指すため，関係代名詞 which に置き換わる．さらに関係詞が節の初めの位置へ移動するとき，which だけではなく，より大きな意味的まとまりである in which が移動し，下の英文となる．

「前置詞＋関係代名詞」はこれで 1 つの関係代名詞のまとまりとみることができるため，日本語では前置詞を訳す必要がない場合が多い．さらに「前置詞＋関係代名詞」に使われる関係代名詞は目的格であるため（代名詞であれば "for him" のように，目的格がくるのは明らかである），「前置詞＋whom（who は不可）」か「前置詞＋which」の形しかない（「前置詞＋that」は不可）．

Exercise 11

1. 次の各句の [ ] で示してある関係節の部分で，意味が足りない部分が主格・目的格・所有格のどの位置かを答え，かっこに適切な関係代名詞を入れなさい（ただし，that は使わないこと）．

1) the man ( ) [I met at Shibuya station]

2) the train ( ) [is bound for Osaka]

3) the woman ( ) [brother is a doctor]

4) the businessman ( ) [is going out for lunch]

5) the watch ( ) [Emily wants to buy]

2. 次の 2 文を，関係代名詞を用いて 1 つの文にしなさい．

1) The man is my uncle.　　　　　You saw him at Sendai.

2) I will go to the village.　　　　My father was born at the village.

3) The mountain is Mt. Fuji.　　　Its top is covered with snow.

4) Do you know the man?　　　　He is sitting on the sofa.

5) I want to give her something.　She doesn't have it.

6) He is the only person.   I can trust him.

7) I remember the day.   I first visited England on the day.

8) The movie was very boring.   You recommended the movie.

3. それぞれの日本文を英語に訳しなさい.

1) 彼はかせいだ金はすべて貯金する.

2) これがベストセラーになった本です.

3) わたしは，先日（the other day）あなたが話をしていた女の子に会った.

4) トムが話していた女性は警察官だった.

覚えておきたい英単語　**11** 社会問題・犯罪

いじめ	bullying
いやがらせ	harassment
セクハラ	sexual harassment
幼児虐待	child abuse
誘拐・拉致	kidnap
麻薬中毒	drug addiction
酒気帯び運転	drunken driving
ひき逃げ事件	hit-and-run case
賄賂	bribe
詐欺	fraud
万引き	shoplift
盗聴	wiretapping / bugging
条例	regulation
違法駐輪の自転車	illegally parked bicycle

第12章　関係詞（2）　関係副詞等

関係副詞

関係副詞も，第11章の関係代名詞と同じ関係詞であるため，関係詞を取り除くとそのうしろの部分に必ず意味的に足りない部分が生じる．

John will visit Tokyo where his grandparents are living .

→関係詞 "where" を取り除くと，□□□ の節は場所を意味する副詞句の部分が不足している．(his grandparents are living _____)

That was the day when he left .

→関係詞 "when" を取り除くと，□□□ の節は時を意味する副詞句の部分が不足している．(he left _____)

このように，場所，時，理由などの意味の部分が関係詞になったものを**関係副詞**（**relative adverb**）といい，関係副詞となった部分は，意味的に不足する要素となる．

関係副詞の基本形

先行詞	場所	時	理由	方法
関係副詞	where	when	why	how

> **注意**
>
> 関係副詞の "why" と "how" に関しては，先行詞と関係副詞が同時に文の中に現れることはあまりなく，どちらか一方が省略されていることが多い．
>
> Tell me the reason ~~why~~ you cannot come to my house.
>
> (関係副詞 why の省略)
>
> Tell me ~~the reason~~ why you cannot come to my house.
>
> (先行詞 the reason の省略)
>
> Show me the way ~~how~~ you did it.　　(関係副詞 how の省略)
>
> Show me ~~the way~~ how you did it.　　(先行詞 the way の省略)

50

関係代名詞と関係副詞の違い

関係代名詞と関係副詞の違いは，関係節の中で関係詞を取り除いた時に意味的に足りない要素が生じる位置の違いにある．

(a)　This is the village <u>where</u> I want to live.

(b)　This is the village <u>which</u> attracts me most.

(a) の文の関係節の部分 "where I want to live" では，場所を表す意味の部分が足りない (I want to live _____)．一方で，(b) の文の関係節の部分 "which attracts me most" では，主格の意味の部分が足りない (_____ attracts me most)．**つまり，関係代名詞と関係副詞のどちらが適切かについては，先行詞で決まるのではなく，うしろの関係節のどの部分が意味的に不足しているのかによって決まる．**

ポイント

関係代名詞か関係副詞かを決めるポイントは，関係節の中の意味的に不足している部分が

① 主格，目的格，所有格の場合は　　　……関係代名詞

② 場所，日時などの副詞句の位置の場合は　……関係副詞

関係副詞と「前置詞＋関係代名詞」

次の2つの文を，関係詞を使って1つの文にする場合，方法は2通り存在する．

$\begin{cases} \text{1980 is the year.} \\ \text{My parents got married in the year.} \end{cases}$

(1)　1980 is the year.　　　　+　　　My parents got married (in) the year .

(in) which

1980 is the year in which my parents got married.

51

"My parents got married in the year." の "the year" の部分を関係詞とする場合，この位置は目的格の位置なので関係代名詞 which を使う.

(2)　1980 is the year.　＋　My parents got married (in) the year .

　　　　　　　　　　　　　　　　　　　　　　　　　　when

　　1980 is the year when my parents got married.

"My parents got married in the year." の "in the year" の部分を関係詞とする場合，この位置は副詞句の位置なので関係副詞 when を使う.
　つまり，「**前置詞＋関係代名詞**」＝「**関係副詞**」とおおむね考えてよく，この2つの間には次の表のような対応関係がある.

関係副詞と前置詞＋関係代名詞の対応関係

先行詞	場所	時	理由	方法
関係副詞	where	when	why	how
前置詞＋ 関係代名詞	at which in which 　　　　など	at which in which 　　　　など	for which 　　　　など	in which 　　　　など

Exercise 12

1. 次の各句の [ ] で示してある関係節の部分で，意味が足りない部分が主格・所有格・目的格・副詞句のどの位置かを答え，かっこに適切な関係代名詞，または関係副詞を入れなさい（ただし，関係代名詞 that は使わないこと）.

1)　the place (　　　　) [the beautiful houses are]

2)　the time (　　　　) [we must finish our reports]

3)　the library (　　　　) [we visit to look for the book]

4)　the reason (　　　　) [he is angry]

2. 次の各組の英文がほぼ同じ意味になるように，（ ）に適語を入れなさい.

1)　(a)　This is the company where my father works.

　　(b)　This is the company (　　　) (　　　) my father works.

52

2) (a) Tell me the reason why you look happy.

  (b) Tell me the reason (　　　) (　　　) you look happy.

3) (a) September is the month when I was born.

  (b) September is the month (　　　) (　　　) I was born.

4) (a) This is how I solved the problem.

  (b) This is the way (　　　) (　　　) I solved the problem.

3. 次の2文を，「前置詞＋関係代名詞」と「関係副詞」を用いて1つの文に
した文をそれぞれ書きなさい．

1) This is the way.   The accident happened in the way.

2) We will stay at the hotel.   A lot of people want to go to the hotel.

3) I remember the day.   I first came to Tokyo on the day.

4) I can't understand the reason.   She left her house for the reason.

5) Do you know the exact time?   The math class starts at the time.

覚えておきたい 英単語　⓬ 企業・会社

ゼネコン	general contractor
公団	public corporation
第三セクター	quasi-public corporation
特殊法人	government-affiliated corporation
中小企業	small business
取引先	customer
ベンチャー企業	start up / venture business
合併	merger
倒産	bankruptcy
提携	cooperation
株主	stockholder

第**13**章　関係詞（3）　その他の応用的用法

関係詞の制限用法と継続用法

一般的に先行詞と関係詞の間にカンマ（,）がないものを**制限用法**（**restrictive use**），カンマ（,）があるものを**継続用法**（**non-restrictive use**）という.

John has a son who is a dentist.（制限用法）
「ジョンには歯医者の息子がいる.」（他に息子がいる可能性あり）
John has a son, who is a dentist.（継続用法）
「ジョンには息子がいて,その息子は歯医者である.」（息子は一人しかいない）

ただし，これらの 2 つの間には英文の生成過程に差がみられる.

制限用法の場合

(a)　John has a son.　　＋

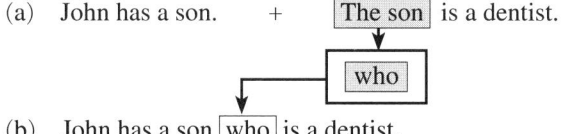

(b)　John has a son who is a dentist.

制限用法の場合は，(a) において "The son is a dentist." の "The son" の部分（主格）が関係詞になるため，関係代名詞 who に変化して 1 文となり (b) の文となる.

継続用法の場合

(a)　John has a son.　　＋　And the son is a dentist.

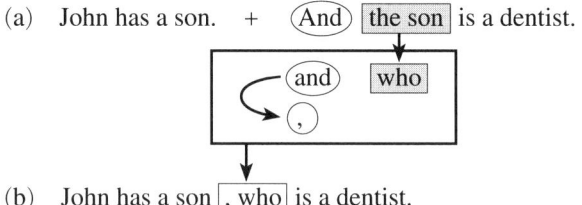

(b)　John has a son , who is a dentist.

一方，継続用法の場合は，(a) において "And the son is a dentist." の "the son" の部分（主格）が関係代名詞 who に変化するまでは制限用法と同じだが，**その後 "and" と "who" がセットで "カンマ（,）＋who" になって (b) の文が生成される**.

したがって，英文上関係詞の制限用法と継続用法には違いがみられないが，継続用法に含まれているカンマ（,）が and や but などの接続詞の役割があるので，**継続用法の関係節は先行詞の補足情報を与える役割を果たす**．

注意

① 関係詞の中で，関係代名詞 that, what, 関係副詞 how, why は継続用法では用いることができない．

② 継続用法の which は，名詞以外の品詞や前の文全体を先行詞とすることができる．

She is <u>modest</u>, which I wants human beings to be. （先行詞が形容詞）

「彼女は謙虚であるが，私は，人間はそうあって欲しいと思う.」

<u>I kept silent</u>, which made him angry. （先行詞が文全体）

「私は黙ったままでいたが，そのことが彼を怒らせた.」

複合関係詞

「関係代名詞（または関係副詞）＋ever」の形をしているものを，**複合関係詞**（**compound relative**）と呼ぶ．複合関係詞の意味は，次のように 2 通りの意味がある．

① 「～でも」

$\boxed{\text{Whatever}}$ you say must be true.

「あなたが言うことは<u>何でも</u>本当に違いない.」

② 「～であっても」（譲歩）（「no mater＋関係詞」に書き換えが可能）

$\boxed{\text{Whatever}}$ you may say, I will not change my opinion.

＝ $\boxed{\text{No matter what}}$ you may say, I will not change my opinion.

「あなたの言うことが<u>何であろうとも</u>，私は意見を変えない.」

注意

複合関係副詞 however に関しては主に譲歩の意味で使われ，語順が「however＋形容詞＋主語＋動詞」になる．

$\boxed{\text{However}}$ hard I try, I can't watch the white bear because of the crowds.

55

疑似関係代名詞の as と but

本来接続詞である as と but が関係代名詞のように使われることがあるが，使われ方が限られている．

・**as**：次の連語の形で as が現れる．
「such A as B」　　　「B するような A」
「the same A as B」　　「B と同じ A」

I want to buy the same car as you have.

・**but**：「not（否定の意味）＋but」の形で現れ，**二重否定の意味になる**．

There is no choice but takes this bus.

Exercise 13

1. 次の英文を日本語に訳しなさい．
1) Please wait till five, when my brother will be back.
2) I first flew to Moscow, where I was going to make connections.
3) Jim said Mary was sick, which was a lie.
4) We should ask him, who is a specialist for the problem.
5) Tom, whose father is a pianist, is bad at playing the piano.

2. 次の各組の英文がほぼ同じ意味になるように，（　）に適語を入れなさい．
1) (a) We can go at any time when you are ready.
　 (b) We can go (　　　) you are ready.
2) (a) I couldn't get the car to start, whatever I did.
　 (b) I couldn't get the car to start, (　　) (　　) (　　) I did.
3) (a) You can choose any of these items that you want.
　 (b) You can choose (　　) (　　) you want.
4) (a) However tired you are, please keep on smiling.
　 (b) (　　) (　　) (　　) tired you are, please keep on smiling.
5) (a) Give it to anyone whom you like.
　 (b) Give it to (　　) you like.

56

3. それぞれの日本文を，関係詞を使って英語に訳しなさい.

1) 私は彼が黒板に書くことを何でもノートに書き写した.

2) 例外のない規則はない.

3) 彼女は私に何枚か DVD を貸してくれたが，面白くなかった.

覚えておきたい英単語　⒔ 職場・オフィス

従業員	employee
雇用主	employer
新入社員	newcomer
移転する	move (the office)
本店・本社	headquarters / head office
支店・支社	branch office
営業課	sales section
会計課	accountant section
人事課	personnel section
総務課	general affairs section
人事異動	personnel changes
部長	general manager
課長	section manager
係長	subsection chief
上司	boss
同僚	colleague
部下	subordinate

第14章　まとめ（1）　文の種類

文の種類

　文は2つの異なる観点から分類することができる．1つ目は意味の上から1. 平叙文，2. 疑問文，3. 命令文，4. 感嘆文の4種類に分けられ，感嘆文以外はいずれも肯定文と否定文がある．一方構造によって，1. 単文，2. 重文，3. 複文に分けることができる．

1.　意味上の分類

1)　平叙文（declarative sentence）

　　　Tom was a member of baseball club.

　　　He is not a member any more.

2)　疑問文（interrogative sentence）

　疑問文には次の4種類がある．音調にも注意が必要である．

a.　一般疑問文（yes-no 疑問文）

　一般疑問文の音調はふつう上昇調である．

　　　Are you a student at this school? — Yes, I am./No, I'm not.

　否定疑問文は否定を含む語がやや強調され，驚きなどの感情の意味合いが付加される．

　　　Aren't you a student at this school?（驚き）— No, I'm not.

b.　特殊疑問文（wh 疑問文）

　特殊疑問文の音調はふつう下降調である．

　　　Why did you come here yesterday?

　　　Why didn't you come here yesterday?（非難）

c.　選択疑問文

　　　Are you coming today or tomorrow?

　　　Aren't you coming today or tomorrow?（苛立ち）

　選択疑問文は音調によって一般疑問文にもなる．

　　　Are you coming today or tomorrow?— No, I'll be here this Friday.

58

d. 付加疑問文

You have a part-time job, don't you? （軽い問いかけ）

— Yes. I'm working at McDonald's.

— No. I'm trying to find one.

You have a part-time job, don't you? （相手に同意を期待する）

— Yes. I'm busy every evening.

e. 間接疑問文：主文は疑問形ではないので上昇調の音調はない.

I know where Mary originally comes from.

I don't know where her husband comes from, though.

Do you know where he comes from? （文自体は疑問文なので上昇調）

— I have no idea.

参考

Where do you think he comes from? （"do you think" が挿入されている）

— I guess he's from Ohio.

3) 命令文 (imperative sentence)

命令, 要求, 依頼, 指示や禁止を表す. ふつう主語 (you) が省略されて, 動詞の原形が文頭に来る. 文末はピリオドで終わるが, 語調が強い場合は感嘆符 (!) が用いられることもある. 音調は下降調である.

a. 肯定の命令文

動詞の原形で始める. please を使うと丁寧な命令文になる.

Be quiet!

Please be seated.

b. 否定の命令文

don't あるいは never で始める.

Don't be late.

Never mind.

c. 使役の命令文

使役動詞 let を用い, 1 人称と 3 人称に対する命令文になる.

let us の短縮形 let's を使うと勧誘表現になる.

Let it go.

Let me help you.

Let's have a party.

Don't let me go.

4) 感嘆文 (**exclamatory sentence**)

喜び，悲しみ，驚きなどの強い感情を表す文で，音調は下降調になる．what や how で始まり，感嘆符 (!) で終わる．

a. What a (an) ＋形容詞＋名詞＋S＋V …!
   What a nice jacket you've got at the flea market today!
b. How＋形容詞（または副詞）＋S＋V …!
   How stupid I am!
   How deeply I miss you!

2. 構造上の分類

文は SV 構造が基本だが，SV 構造が 1 つである場合と，2 つ以上の SV 構造がある場合，相互の関係によって分類され，1) 単文　2) 重文　3) 複文 に分けられる．

1) 単文 (**simple sentence**)

SV 構造を 1 つしか持たない文を**単文**という．

I do laundry every weekend.   [単文]

2) 重文 (**compound sentence**)

SV 構造が 2 つ以上あり，それが and, but, or, for 等の接続詞によって対等な関係で結ばれている文を**重文**という．

I do laundry and my husband cooks dinner every weekend.   [重文]

3) 複文 (**complex sentence**)

SV 構造が 2 つ以上あり，そのうちの 1 つが意味上で主要な節（主節）となり，他の節（従属節）は主節を意味的に補う働きをする文を**複文**という．従属節は名詞節，形容詞節，副詞節に分類される（第 15 章参照）．

I do laundry after I come back from my Yoga lesson every weekend.

                                                               [複文]

※ライティングの際には，単文ばかりではなく，重文，複文のバリエーションを意識して文を書くことが大切である．

60

Exercise 14

1. 次の各文を疑問文に書き換えなさい.

1) You were late for school yesterday.
2) Tom forgot to do his homework.
3) Mary needs to open an account at the bank.
4) You think it is a waste of money.
5) You can't wait until tomorrow.

2. 次の各文を（　）内の構造の文に書き換えなさい.

1) Arriving early in the morning, I enjoyed walking around the station.（複文）
2) When I was eighteen, I met my future husband.　（単文）
3) I like to do the dishes, but I hate to cook for myself.　（複文）
4) I believe that the rumor will disappear pretty soon.（surely を用いて単文）
5) Our flight was delayed due to the bad weather in Tokyo.　（複文）

覚えておきたい
英単語　**14** 配達・輸送

小型トラック	pickup
貨物	freight
貨物トラック	truck / lorry（英）
送料	shipping charge
宅配便	delivery service / courier
段ボール箱	cardboard box
ガムテープ	packing tape / masking tape
料金前払い	advance payment
料金着払い	cash on delivery / payment on arrival
速達	express service
割れ物	fragile article
書留郵便	registered mail

第15章 句と節

　文を構成する最も小さな要素は「語」であるが，いくつかの語が集まって，1つの名詞・形容詞・副詞に相当する働きをするのが**句**（**phrase**）と**節**（**clause**）である．2つ以上の語が主部と述部の構造を持っていれば「節」，持たない場合は「句」と分類される．

句の分類

1. 名詞句（noun phrase）

　文中で名詞に相当する働きをし，文の主語・補語・目的語になる．動詞の変化形では主に不定詞および動名詞が名詞句になる．

> It is difficult to finish the homework by tomorrow . （to 不定詞句）
> I promised not to break the rules . （to 不定詞句）
> You should learn how to use the PC . （疑問詞＋to 不定詞句）
> Learning English is important for students. （動名詞）
> My hobby is playing the guitar . （動名詞）
> I look forward to seeing you at the meeting . （動名詞）

2. 形容詞句（adjective phrase）

　文中で形容詞に相当する働きをし，名詞，代名詞を修飾したり，補語になる．動詞の変化形では主に不定詞，分詞，また「前置詞＋名詞句」が形容詞句となる．

> Would you like something to drink ? （to 不定詞）
> Look at the animals dancing to the music . （現在分詞）
> The books in the library are in order. （前置詞＋名詞句）

3. 副詞句（adverb phrase）

　文中で副詞に相当する働きをし，動詞，形容詞，副詞や文全体を修飾する．動詞の変化形では主に不定詞，分詞構文，また「前置詞＋名詞句」が副詞句となる．

> I started a part-time job to earn some extra money . （to 不定詞句）
> Considering all the facts , I decided to continue my efforts. （分詞構文）

I'll see you tomorrow at the airport . （前置詞＋名詞句）

I'm so glad to have you here as a special guest . （to 不定詞句）

節の分類

1. 名詞節 （noun clause）

文中で名詞に相当する働きをし，**that 節**に導かれ，文の主語・補語・目的語および同格節になる.

It is required that each of us bring our own identification card . （主語）

The fact is that Mary never comes on time . （補語）

The research shows that the population of Japan is decreasing . （目的語）

I heard the news that we won't be able to join the event any more . （同格）

2. 形容詞節 （adjective clause）

文中で形容詞に相当する働きをし，関係詞によって導かれ（これを関係節という），先行詞である名詞・代名詞を修飾する.

Please show me the map which covers all the famous spots in this town .

I have a friend whose brother is a famous musician in the U.S.

Do you remember the woman (whom) you met at the party ?

This is the place where we are going to have a meeting this month .

3. 副詞節 （adverb clause）

文中で時，原因・理由，目的・結果，条件等を表す部分（従属節）として，文の中心となる部分（主節）を修飾する働きをする.

When I was a freshman at college , I met my wife in English class.

My mother has never been abroad as she is afraid of taking an airplane .

I was so surprised that I closed the door immediately .

If you want to make a good speech , practice and confidence are the keys to success.

63

Exercise 15

1. 次の英文を読み，名詞句，形容詞句，副詞句，名詞節，形容詞節，副詞節を１つずつ書き出しなさい．

When you think of something to require willpower, what's the first thing that comes to mind? For most of us, the classic test of willpower is resisting temptation, whether the temptress is a doughnut, a cigarette, a clearance sale, or a one-night stand. When people say, "I have no willpower," what they usually mean is, "I have trouble saying no when my mouth, stomach, heart want to say yes." (McGonigal, K. The Willpower Instinct, 2012)

名詞句：
形容詞句：
副詞句：
名詞節：
形容詞節：
副詞節：

2. 次の各文の下線部の句または節の種類を書き，全体の日本語訳を書きなさい．(McGonigal, K. The Willpower Instinct, 2012 より引用)
1) This was just the beginning of the need for <u>what we now call willpower.</u>
(willpower: 意志力)
2) Our modern power of self-control is the product of long-ago pressures <u>to be better neighbors, parents, and mates.</u>
3) Robert Sapolsky, a neurobiologist at Stanford University, has argued that the main job of the modern prefrontal cortex <u>is to bias the brain.</u>
(neurobiologist: 神経生物学者, prefrontal cortex: 前頭葉)

3. 次の各文を（　）内の句または節を使って英語で書きなさい．
1) ヤンキースが勝つとは思わなかった． （名詞句）
2) 村上春樹の著書は世界中で知られている． （形容詞句）
3) 現状を鑑みると，国内に残るのが無難だ． （副詞句）

64

4) 妹に鳥取の砂の美術館に行くように勧めた. （名詞節）

5) あなたが面白いと思う本を教えてもらえますか？ （形容詞節）

6) 流暢な英語を話せるようになりたいなら，英語で日記をつけなさい.

（副詞節）

覚えておきたい英単語　15 国際問題

貿易摩擦	trade conflicts
経済危機	financial crisis
経済援助	economic support
経済制裁	economic sanctions
平和外交	peaceful diplomacy
軍隊派遣	dispatching troops
軍隊撤退	withdrawal / evacuation of troops
外交官	diplomat
大使館	embassy
大使	ambassador
条約	treaty
核軍縮	nuclear arms reduction / nuclear disarmament

65

第16章　接続詞と文の接続

接続詞（**conjunction**）は文中の語と語，句と句，節と節とを結びつける．文法上対等の関係にあるものを結ぶのが**等位接続詞**（**coordinate conjunction**），従属節を主節に結びつけるのが**従属接続詞**（**subordinate conjunction**）である．接続詞ではないが，等位接続詞と同じ働きをする**接続副詞**（**conjunctive adverb**）の用法も大切である．

接続詞の種類 1：機能的分類

1. 等位接続詞（coordinate conjunction）

語と語，句と句，節と節（文と文）のように同じ種類のものを対等の関係で結ぶ：and, but, or ...

語＋語　　I learned French and German.

句＋句　　When are you going to have a meeting, in the morning or (in the) afternoon?

節＋節　　I caught a cold, so I was absent from school.

※接続副詞（conjunctive adverb）

品詞は副詞だが，等位接続詞のように2つの節，文をつなぐ働きをする：besides, moreover, however, nevertheless, therefore ...

Study hard, otherwise , you will fail the class. （**1文中の節と節**）

I was late for school. Moreover , I forgot my homework. （**文と文**）

2. 従属接続詞（subordinate conjunction）

節（S＋V）と節（S＋V）を主と従の関係で結ぶ．

66

(1)　従属節が名詞節の場合

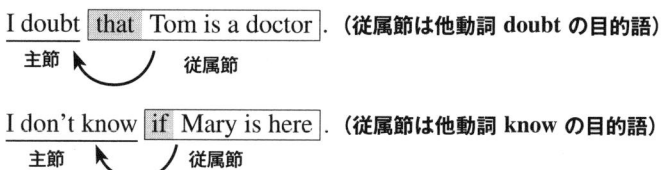

I doubt that Tom is a doctor . （従属節は他動詞 **doubt** の目的語）
主節　　　　　　　従属節

I don't know if Mary is here . （従属節は他動詞 **know** の目的語）
主節　　　　　　　従属節

(2)　従属節が副詞節の場合

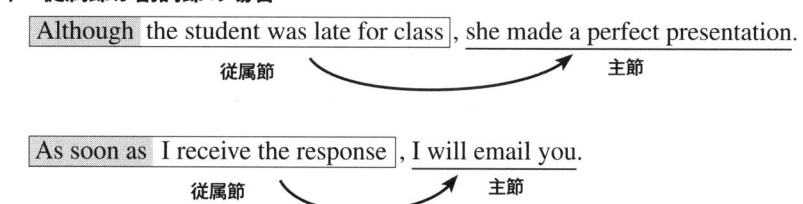

Although the student was late for class , she made a perfect presentation.
　　　　　　従属節　　　　　　　　　　　　　　主節

As soon as I receive the response , I will email you.
　　　　従属節　　　　　　　　　　　　　主節

接続詞の種類 2 : 形態的分類

1.　単純接続詞（**simple conjunction**）

1語でできているもの：and, but, or, when, if, as, because, for …

You and I are in the same boat.

2.　接続詞句（**conjunction phrase**）

数語が集まって 1 つの接続詞の働きをするもの：as soon as, as long as, even though, as if, by the time …

Even though I do not have much time to read, I never skip my habit of reading.

3.　相関接続詞（**correlative conjunction**）

一対の語句が対応して接続詞の働きをするもの：both A and B, either A or B, neither A nor B, not only A but also B, so ... that S + V …

I have a part-time job on both Tuesdays and Fridays.
The actress is neither beautiful nor talented.

67

接続詞と前置詞の書き換え

従属接続詞によってつながれた2つの節から成り立つ文を前置詞を使って単文に書き換えることができる.

Because the flight was delayed, we could not attend the party.
→ Due to the delayed flight, we could not attend the party.

Although it snowed heavily, I managed to go out to town.
→ In spite of heavy snow, I managed to go out to town.

While I was staying in the US, I wanted to visit Lincoln Center.
→ During my stay in the US, I wanted to visit Lincoln Center.

Exercise 16

1. 各文の（　）で適当なものを選び, 接続詞の種類を, ア〜ウから選んで答えなさい.

1) (As / If) you need more information, please visit our web site.

2) Please turn off the air conditioner (before / until) you leave the room.

3) (According to / Due to) the white paper, half of the respondents remain single.

4) Ms. Kato won't use her umbrella (however / even if) it rains heavily.

5) The shop is conveniently located at the corner (and / but) across from the library.

6) You had better study harder, (otherwise / however), you will fail the exam scheduled for next month.

7) Employees who wish to develop their skills should join this seminar just (after / while) they start working at the company.

8) (Whether / As) you like it or not doesn't matter.

（ア．等位接続詞, イ．従属接続詞, ウ．接続副詞）

68

2. 次の各文を英語に訳しなさい.

1) コーヒーか紅茶かどちらかをいただきます.

2) 昨日はとても疲れていたので, 外出しなかった.

3) 中学の頃, テニス部に入っていた.

4) 今朝寝坊をした. それでいつもの電車に乗り遅れた.

5) 大学が4月に始まるまでアルバイトをするつもりだ.

覚えておきたい
英単語

16 文具類など

文具類	stationery
マジックペン	marker
ボールペン	ballpoint
シャープペン	mechanical pencil
消しゴム	eraser
クリアファイル	folder
定規	ruler
ものさし	measure
ノート	notebook
貼り紙・ビラ	notice
メモ・備忘録	memorandum
メモ帳	memo pad
メモ用紙	memo paper
ホッチキス	stapler
郵便物の重量計	letter scale
のり	glue, paste
棚	shelves
セロテープ	Scotch tape
シール	sticker

第**17**章　不定詞 (to 不定詞・原形不定詞)

不定詞とは

　不定詞（**infinitive**）は準動詞の１つであり，大部分の不定詞は "to do" のように to をつけて，**to 不定詞**（**to-infinitive**）と言われる．to のつかない不定詞は**原形不定詞**（**bare infinitive**）と言われる．それぞれ，文の中で不定詞（句）がどのような機能を果たしているのかを見極めることにより，用法を具体的に捉えることができる．

to 不定詞の分類

　to 不定詞は大別すると I 名詞的用法，II 形容詞的用法，III 副詞的用法の 3 種類になる．文における不定詞（句）の位置と他の要素との関係に注目をすると，その働きが捉えやすい．

　to 不定詞の基本用法を文構造の観点から概観する．

I　名詞的用法：～すること

　to 不定詞句が導く句全体で「～すること」という名詞句を形成するので，基本文型の成分の主語 (S)，補語 (C)，目的語 (O) になることができる．

(1)　to 不定詞句が主語になる

　　 To master these ideas is quite difficult for me.
　　　　　　　S

(2)　to 不定詞句が補語になる

　　 My goal is to master these ideas .
　　　　　　　　　　　　C

(3)　to 不定詞句が目的語になる

　　 I wanted to master these ideas , but found it impossible.
　　　　　　　　　　　　O

(4)　[疑問詞] + to 不定詞句で目的語になる

　　 I would like to know how to master these ideas .
　　　　　　　　　　　　　　　　O

70

II 形容詞的用法：～するための，～すべき等

名詞(句)の後ろから修飾するものである.

(1) 前の名詞(句)が to 不定詞(句)の意味上の主語・目的語になる

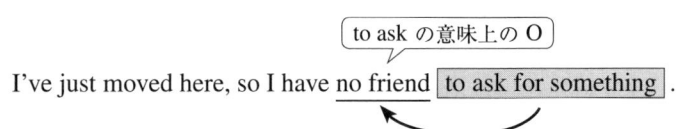

I've just moved here, so I have no friend to ask for something .

(2) to 不定詞(句)が前の名詞(句)と同格の場合

John has a desire to become a famous scientist .

III 副詞的用法：～するために等

to 不定詞句全体が目的・原因などを表す副詞句として機能する.

(1) 目的を表すもの：～するために

I have to check this paper to master these ideas .

(2) 原因を表すもの：～すると…

She was really glad to hear the news that John has passed the exam .

※この場合,感情を示す語が不定詞句の直前にあるという位置関係になっている.
不定詞句の内容が感情を引き起こす原因となる.

(3) 理由を表すもの：～するなんて

You must be happy to have a lot of friends to support you .

(4) 慣用的に独立して用いられるもの（独立不定詞）

・**to tell the truth: 実を言うと**

To tell the truth , we haven't finished our report yet.

・**needless to say: 言うまでもなく**

Needless to say , we have to consider our financial situation first.

※他に, **strange to say**：奇妙なことに, **so to speak**：いわば 等がある.

原形不定詞

原形不定詞は，主として，(1) 使役動詞 (make, let, have 等)，(2) 知覚動詞
(see, hear, feel 等) と共に用いられる.

71

（1）　使役動詞と共に用いる：**S＋V＋O＋原形不定詞「S が O に〜させる」**

The teacher made the students clean their classroom .

　　　　　　　　　　⌐→ The students cleaned their classroom

　目的語 O "the students" と原形不定詞 "clean" との間には，主述関係が成立している（"The students cleaned their classroom." という文が内包されている）．

（2）　知覚動詞と共に用いる：**S＋V＋O＋原形不定詞「S が，O が〜するのを見る／聞く／感じる」**

John saw the students enter the movie theater .

　　　　　⌐→ The students entered the movie theater.

　使役動詞の場合と同様，文中の目的語 O と原形不定詞との間には，主述関係が成立している（"The students entered the movie theater."）．
　使役動詞，知覚動詞いずれにも言えることだが，主述関係を理解しないと，「原形不定詞句で示された行為が誰によって行われるのか」という点を見過ごすので，要注意である．詳しくは第 22 章で述べる．

Exercise 17

1. 下線部の不定詞の用法を「名詞的用法，形容詞的用法，副詞的用法」から選び，全文を日本語に訳しなさい．

1) It was careless of you to try to enter the room without a pass.

2) John had nothing to do today, so he spent all afternoon reading a novel.

3) Everyone in the classroom was surprised at his decision to quit school.

4) We are really sorry to hear that your grandmother passed away.

5) He is facing a lot of challenges, but he has the patience to overcome them.

2. 下線部の原形不定詞の意味上の主語を答えなさい．

1) She had the dentist look at one of her teeth to be relieved from its pain.

2) Let the boy explain his opinion that he needs some money to get the item.

3) After the storm has passed, my father made me clean the window.

3. 与えられた日本語の意味に合うように，[ ] 内の語(句)を並べ替えなさい．ただし，文頭は大文字で始めること．

1) 言うまでもなく，運動の前には適度な準備運動が必要です．

[moderate / needless / , / need / say / warming-up / you / to] before exercising.

2) 緊張のせいで，心臓が激しく鼓動するのを感じた．

[my / fast / felt / heart / I / beat] due to getting nervous.

3) ここにいる誰もが，その機械の操作方法を思い出せなかった．

Everyone around here [operate / how / remember / the machine / couldn't / to].

4) 奇妙なことに，昨日落とした財布が突然見付かった．

[say / I / yesterday / to / the wallet / , / strange / lost] has just been found.

覚えておきたい英単語　17 事務処理・面接

書類	documents
書式	form / format
履歴書	curriculum vitae
記入	entry
(書類に) 記入する	fill in
応募する	apply
応募	application
推薦状	letter of recommendation
就職面接	job interview
候補者	candidate
面接官	interviewer
採用	adaptation / acceptance
ハローワーク	employment service / job security office

第18章 分詞（現在分詞・過去分詞・分詞構文）

分詞とは

分詞（**participle**）は，不定詞と同様に準動詞の1つであり，(1)**現在分詞**（**present participle**），(2)**過去分詞**（**past participle**）の2つがある．ここでは，現在分詞・過去分詞の基本用法を概観し，応用的な表現である**分詞構文**を説明する．

分詞の用法

現在分詞，過去分詞ともに単独であれば前から（前置修飾），目的語，前置詞句などを伴っていれば後ろから修飾（後置修飾）する．基本的に，現在分詞は「能動」，過去分詞は「受動」の意味を持つ．

I 現在分詞：〜している

(1)分詞単独で前から，(2)他の語(句)を伴っていれば後ろから名詞(句)を修飾する．

(1) Please look at the running dog.

(2) Please look at the dog running in the park.

この文構造は，過去分詞を用いた場合でも同様である．

II 過去分詞：〜られた／られている

通常，受動態の意味でターゲットの名詞(句)を修飾する．

(1) Watch out for the broken glass.

(2) Watch out for the glass broken by the typhoon.

S＋V＋分詞

分詞の叙述用法とも呼ばれ，第2文型SVCにおいて補語Cが分詞の場合

を指す. この場合は, 状態や動作の継続を示す keep, remain の他, sit, stand 等と共に使われる場合が多い.

John kept running on the racetrack for thirty minutes.
　S　　　　C

☞ John ran on the racetrack for thirty minutes.

My grandfather sat surrounded by his grandchildren.
　　S　　　　　　C

☞ My grandfather was surrounded by his grandchildren.

この構文において, 主語 S と補語 C（分詞）の間に主述関係が成立するが, その際, 能動／受動のどちらの関係になっているのかを見定める必要がある. 能動であれば現在分詞, 受動であれば過去分詞である.

▌S＋V＋O＋分詞

第5文型 SVOC において補語 C が分詞である場合は, 目的語 O と補語 C（分詞）の間に主述関係が成立する. 現在分詞／過去分詞の選択は「S＋V＋分詞」の構文と同様の注意が必要となる.

They kept me waiting at the bus stop for thirty minutes last night.
　　　　O　　C

☞ I waited at the bus stop for thirty minutes last night.

I heard my name called in the distance.
　　　　O　　　C

☞ My name was called in the distance.

▌分詞構文

分詞構文（**participial construction**）は, 従属節「接続詞＋S＋V」のユニットを分詞に置き換えて, 文を簡潔にするためのものである.
以下に, 従属節を分詞構文に変換する場合の手順と要点を示す.

When John arrived at the station , he found that the train had already left.
　　　　　⬇
Arriving at the station , John（＝he）found that the train had already left.

75

> 手順 ① 主節の主語と従属節の主語が同一であることを確認する.
> ② 従属節の主語を削除する.
> ③ 接続詞を削除する.
> ④ 従属節に残った動詞を分詞に置き換える.（上記の場合 arrived → arriving）

　分詞構文は，元の従属節の接続詞の意味に従って，時（〜する時），条件（〜するなら），譲歩（〜する一方で），原因（〜することで），理由（〜するので），付帯状況（〜しながら）等の意味で解釈される．**分詞構文では元の従属節の接続詞が明示した意味が示されないので，特に注意が必要である.**

独立分詞構文

　元になる文で，主節と従属節の主語が異なる場合,分詞構文生成の手順（上図）で ② は適用されず，分詞の前に主語が置かれる構文となる．この様な分詞構文を**独立分詞構文**（**absolute participial construction**）という．意味解釈は通常の分詞構文と同じである.

　Since it was Sunday , the shopping mall was crowded with many people.

　⬇

　It being Sunday , the shopping mall was crowded with many people.

その他の重要な分詞構文

(1) 完了形の分詞構文（主節より前の時を指示）
　Having visited many times , I knew what would happen next.

(2) 過去分詞の分詞構文（受動態の場合）
　Seen from the airplane , the rock looked like a whale.

(3) 慣用的な分詞構文

・**speaking of 〜：〜と言えば，〜について言えば**
　Speaking of him , I wonder if he is going well.

・**judging from/of 〜：〜から判断して**
　Judging from what he said, we have to reconsider our relationship with him.

・**frankly speaking：率直に言うと**
　Frankly speaking , I don't like her way of speaking.

・**strictly speaking：厳密に言うと**
　Strictly speaking , your words are not suitable for the situation.

Exercise 18

1. それぞれの英文の下線部を分詞構文に置き換えて，全文を日本語に訳しなさい．

　1) <u>When I was in this town</u>, I always felt that all the people were very friendly to strangers.

　2) <u>As I had not had such an experience</u>, I did't know what I should do.

　3) <u>Since there was no useful information</u>, we had to check the data again.

　4) This bullet train leaves Hakata at 10:00, <u>and arrives at Nagoya at 12:30.</u>

2. それぞれの日本文の全文を英語に訳しなさい．ただし，下線部があるものについては分詞構文を用いること．

　1) 図書館で勉強しているあの少年は，私のいとこです．

　2) 私は，店でその商品が売り切れたことに気づいた．

　3) <u>厳密に言うと</u>，英語では「水」と「お湯」の表現には違いがある．

覚えておきたい英単語　**18 書籍・出版・学術論文**

本の部数	number of copies
出版	publication
初版	first edition
著作権	copyright
学術雑誌	academic journal
学会誌	bulletin
査読者	reviewer / referee
採択	acceptance
不採択	rejection
研究論文	paper
学位論文	thesis
博士論文	doctoral dissertation

第19章　動名詞

動名詞の機能

　動名詞（**gerund**）は動詞から派生した名詞であり，「〜すること」と典型的に訳される．-ing の語尾を持つが（going < go, having < have など），これは現在分詞（present participle）と同形であるので注意が必要である．

① 名詞の性質：動詞と名詞の性質を合わせ持つことから，名詞と同様，文中で主語，補語，目的語のはたらきをしたり，前置詞の目的語となったりする．

　　Understanding trigonometric functions is crucial for mathematics learning.
　　　　　　　　　　　　　　　　　　　　　　　　　　　　　　（主語のはたらき）

　　My favorite hobby is listening to music.　　　　　（補語のはたらき）

　　　　cf: He was listening to the radio when his father came home.
　　　　　　　　　　　　　　　　　　　　　　　　（listening は現在分詞）

　　He likes traveling abroad.　　　　　　　　　　　　（目的語のはたらき）

　　I'm interested in using SNS.　　　　　　（前置詞の目的語のはたらき）

② 動詞の性質：目的語や補語を取ったり，意味上の主語を伴ったりする．

・目的語を取る．

　　Keeping a promise is highly valued.
　　　　　　keep の目的語

・補語を取る．

　　Becoming an engineer is not easy.
　　　　　　　become の補語

・意味上の主語を伴う．

　　Do you mind my [me] asking some questions?
　　　　　　　　　　　　　　　ask の意味上の主語

　　※意味上の主語は所有格で示すのが原則であるが，名詞の場合は目的格が用いられることがしばしばある．口語では，代名詞の場合にも目的格を用いることが多い．

動名詞のさまざまな形

動名詞を否定する場合は直前に not や never を置く．

Not eating any fruit and vegetables will make you fat.

By never allowing yourself a sense of satisfaction for your achievements you may achieve far less than people with more realistic goals.

動名詞の受動態は "being＋過去分詞" で作り「～されること」，完了形は "having＋過去分詞" で「～だったこと」(述語動詞で示される時より以前の時) となる．

I was frustrated at being treated like a child.

Her mother is proud of having been a member of the university.

動名詞を用いる表現

動名詞を用いる重要な慣用表現が多くある．

- **look forward to ～ing: ～するのを楽しみにする**
  I'm looking forward to seeing you again.
- **cannot help ～ing: ～せずにいられない**
  I cannot help laughing at your idea.
- **on ～ing: ～する時（と同時）に**
  On entering the house, the music started to play.
- **feel like ～ing: ～したい気分である**
  I don't feel like going out today.
- **be used to ～ing: ～するのに慣れている**
  He was not used to living with other people.

動名詞のみを目的語とする動詞

- 次の動詞は不定詞ではなく動名詞を目的語として取る：avoid, enjoy, escape, finish, give up, mind, practice, stop など．
  You should give up smoking.
  Passwords can help us avoid being hacked.

- 不定詞のみを目的語として取る動詞がある：agree, decide, hope, mean, plan, promise, refuse, wish など．
  The captain refused to obey orders to leave the island.

Once we receive your complaint, we promise to contact you within five working days.

・動名詞・不定詞両方を目的語とし，意味の変わらないもの：begin, continue, like, prefer, propose, start など．

He continued working [to work] in the company as a computer specialist for three years.

Why do you prefer playing [to play] video games such as Pokémon Go?

・両方取るが意味の異なるもの：remember, forget, try, regret など．

$\left\{\begin{array}{l}\text{I remember sending a copy of the application form to the college's office.} \\ \text{Please remember to send the e-mail to Richard.}\end{array}\right.$

Exercise 19

1. 次の動詞を動名詞の形に変えなさい．
1) begin   2) make   3) sleep
4) stop   5) watch

2. ［　］内の語句を並べ替えて文を完成させなさい．
1) He is complaining about [assigning / his teacher's / homework / to him / too much].
2) There is no chance of [being / in / successful / the game / you].
3) The mother scolded Judith for [the house / leaving / not / soon].
4) The teacher has regrets for [coming / never / the student / to school].

3. （　）内を動名詞を用いて適当な形に変えて文を完成させなさい．
1) The politician doesn't like (surround) by journalists.
2) She is very angry. How do you feel now about (take) this action without her permission?
3) The old man died after (take) to hospital.
4) I am sorry for not (introduce) myself properly.

4. 日本語に訳しなさい.

1) I remember meeting so many foreign students at the university.

2) Why is statistics useful for learning environmental studies?

3) It is no use making comments about his plan.

4) Russian tourists prefer travelling abroad to domestic tourism.

5. 動名詞を使って英語に訳しなさい.

1) ネット上で日記をつけるのはとても楽しいです.（ネット上で日記をつける：keep a diary online）

2) きみはコンピューターウイルスがコンピューターに広がるのを防がなければなりません.（コンピューターウィルス：computer viruses, 〜が — するのを防ぐ：prevent ~ from —ing）

3) エミリーはイングランドを訪問するのを延期することに決めました.（延期する：put off）

覚えておきたい英単語 ⓳ 銀行・金融

金融	finance
銀行口座	bank account
預金	deposit
預金通帳	bankbook / deposit book
（預金を）引き出す	withdraw
送金する	remit
振り込む	transfer
利子	interest
配当	allotment
印税	royalty
給料	salary
報酬	compensation

第**20**章 　比較表現

原級・比較級・最上級

英語の比較表現には，基本となる**原級 (absolute)** を基に，**比較級 (comparative)**，**最上級 (superlative)** の 3 種類があり，形容詞，副詞がこれらの級に活用する．活用は，大部分の 1 音節および一部の 2 音節の語の場合は，-er, -est をつけ，大部分の 2 音節およびすべての 3 音節以上の語の場合は，活用語尾をつけず，"more" "most" を先行させる．

原級	比較級	最上級	
tall	taller	tallest	（1 音節）
early	earlier	earliest	（2 音節）
careful	more careful	most careful	（2 音節）
international	more international	most international	（5 音節）

同等比較

"as ～ as" の形で，2 つのものの程度が同程度であることを表現する．

　Tom is as tall as Hiroshi.

　Masako swims as fast as Ayumi.

これらの例文における，"tall" "fast" は，「背が（普通より）高い」「（普通より）速く」という意味にはならないことに注意．あくまでも，2 つのもの（人）が "tall" "fast" に対して同程度であって，必ずしも両者とも「背が高い」「速く」というわけではない．

John isn't as tall as Peter.

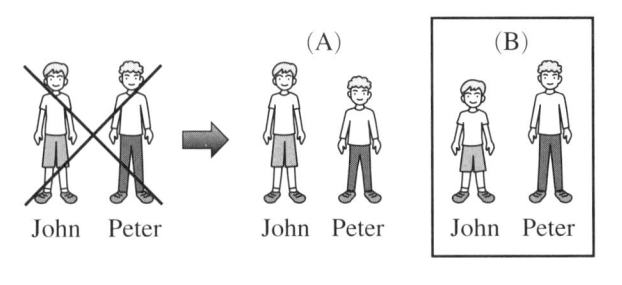

否定の場合は,「同等である」ことを否定するので, 例えば "John isn't as tall as Peter." は, 論理的には, 前ページの (A), (B) の両方が可能であるが, 英語ではおおむね (B) で解釈される.

形容詞が名詞を修飾している場合は語順に注意が必要である.

Nancy wants to have as pretty a doll as Lucy's./Nancy wants to have a doll as pretty as Lucy's.

Masahiko collects as many stamps as Shinji./*Masahiko collects stamps as many as Shinji.（数量詞 "many" "much" は不可）

比較級の構文

一方が他方より程度が高い場合, "比較級 + than" を用いて表現する.

The Lake Towada is wider than the Lake Tazawa.

比較級を強調する場合, "much" "(by) far" は「…よりずっと〜」"still" "even" は「さらに〜」「いっそう〜」となる.

Mt. Fuji is far higher than Mt. Daisen.

In mid January it becomes still colder than in December.

劣等比較

"little" の 比較級 "less" を用いた "less 〜 than" は,「より〜でない」という比較の優劣が逆転した表現となるが, 英語ではあまり多用されない.

To pass the entrance examination of a university, good memory is less important than imagination or creativity.

最上級の構文

あるものが最高の程度であることを表現するとき, "the + 最上級" を用いる. 最上級で表現される対象は, ある集団の中で程度が際立っているという意味で特定されるため, 必ず定冠詞 "the" が付される（副詞にはなくても構わない）.

Bill became the fastest runner in the 100m race in the athletic meeting.

最上級を強調する場合は "much" "by far" を使い,「ずば抜けて」「ダントツで」となる.

Noguchi Hideyo was by far the cleverest boy in the elementary school.

同一のものに関して補語になる場合は "the" は通常つけない.

The view of the Lake Towada is most beautiful from here.

一方，比較級でも「二者のうちで」をともなう場合，定冠詞がつけられる.

Tottori Prefecture has the smaller population of the two prefectures in San'in region.

まぎらわしい more, most

more

・"many" "much" の比較級「より多い／多く」

Men normally eat more food than women.

・比較級を表す "more"

These days society has become more international than that of 30 years ago.

most

・"many" "much" の最上級「最も多い／多く」

In this game the player who collects the most chestnuts is the champion.

・最上級を表す "most"

He is known as the most successful person in the history of the world.

・「ほとんどの」

Most of the audience got bored during the lecture.

Exercise 20

1. 例にならって，それぞれ，同等比較の文を作りなさい.

例：She runs fast. / he → She runs as fast as he.

1) I am tall. / you
2) My uncle could swim fast in his childhood. / my father
3) Masaru likes soba very much. / udon
4) Takao became a famous singer in Japan. / Kenji

2. 例にならって，それぞれ，比較級を使った文を作りなさい.

例：She runs fast. / he → She runs faster than he.

1) My father is old. / my uncle

2) The curry and rice at this restaurant is hot. / that restaurant

3) The architect wanted to build a tall tower. / Tokyo Skytree

4) The athlete ran fast. / the current Japanese record holder

3. 例にならって，それぞれ，最上級を使った文を作りなさい．

例：She runs fast. / three → She runs the fastest of the three.

1) He is tall. / his class

2) The actress in the movie is good. / these ten years

3) He is a great pianist. / the world

4) Mt. Fuji is very high. / Japan

4. 次の日本文を英語に直しなさい．

1) 今年の冬は雪は去年ほど多くない．

2) この本はとても難解で，ほとんどの人は最後まで読み切れない．

3) この賞は，今年もっとも活躍したスポーツ選手に贈られます．

4) 今日は通学バスが昨日よりずっと混んでいる．

覚えておきたい 英単語　**⑳ 差別・平等**

差別	discrimination
平等	equality
逆差別	reverse discrimination
差別用語	discriminatory expression
ポリティカルコレクトネス	political correctness
民族差別	ethnic discrimination
性差別者	sexist
性的区別のない	gender-neutral
身体障害者	physically challenged people / disabled / handicapped
精神障害の	mentally ill
ワスプ	WASP (white Anglo-Saxon Protestant)
愛国者	patriot
狂信的愛国主義者	chauvinist

第21章　受動態

受動態の意味

　ある他動詞文（目的語をともなった文）があったとき，動作の方向性によって異なる表現となる場合，それを動詞の**態**（**voice**）という．動作動詞である他動詞は，動作を行う**動作主**（**agent**）と動作の作用を受ける**被動作主**（**patient**）をともなうが，動作主を主語とする場合を**能動態**（**active voice**），被動作主を主語とする場合を**受動態**（**passive voice**）という．例えば，"chase（追いかける）"という動詞による描写を表す次のイラストは，動作主である"cat（ねこ）"を主語にすると能動態，被動作主である"mouse（ねずみ）"を主語にすると受動態になる．文の表現形式は異なるが，同じイラストの描写であることには変わりはない．

	The cat chases the mouse.	（能動態）
	動作主・主語　　被動作主・目的語	

　The mouse is chased (by the cat).　（受動態）
　被動作主・主語　　　　動作主・前置詞句

能動態の文では動作主"cat"が主語，被動作主"mouse"が目的語である．受動態の文では，能動態の目的語である被動作主"mouse"が主語に昇格し，動詞は **be ＋ 過去分詞**の形を取る．能動態の文の主語であった動作主は，受動態では前置詞句"by 〜"に降格し，文の後方に移動する．

受動文における by 〜 の有無

　受動文の動作主（この場合 "by the cat"）は文の構造上，あってもなくても構わない．以下の例では，あえて"by 〜"は表出されない．

(1)　Unfortunately he was injured in the semi-final match of the judo tournament.

(2)　Murakami Haruki's new novel is now being sold in every bookshop all over Japan.

(1) は，"injure"の動作主が特定不能の場合である．つまり，怪我を与えた動作主がわからないので（必ずしも対戦相手とは限らない），元の能動文が復元

できないのである．(2) は "sell" の動作主は every bookshop の店員か経営者，または本の出版元であるだろうから，(2) のような受動文から能動文を復元する場合，"They sell ～ ." のように，不特定多数を漠然と表現する 3 人称複数の人称代名詞 "they" を使うのが一般的である．しかし，これはかなり不自然な表現である．まして，受動文 (2) のなかで，"by them" のような漠然としたものに対して前置詞句の形式であえて音形をとどめるというのも極めて冗長であり，むしろ不要である．

感情を表す動詞の受動文

"surprise" "satisfy" など，感情を表す動詞は，その感情を発する動作の主体（ここまでの説明の中の「動作主」ではない）を主語にとる受動態で表される．文法上の動作主は，by ～ に限らず，他の前置詞をともなう場合が多い．

The boy was frightened by/at the loud noise.

She was surprised at the unexpected present from the colleagues.

The world-famous painter was never satisfied with the masterpiece.

この種の動詞ではないが，次の動詞も受動文の動作主の前の前置詞が by 以外になる．

Ichiro Suzuki is widely known to American citizens.

Due to yesterday's heavy snow the main street in Aomori city was covered with snow.

After the barbecue the party room was filled with smoky air.

進行形の受動態

→ be being 過去分詞

The new game software is being produced at the factory now.

完了形の受動態

→ have been 過去分詞

The historically important displays in the museum have been lost for

87

over 50 years.

完了進行形の受動態

→ have been being 過去分詞

Sagrada Família started to be constructed in 1882, and it has been being constructed ever since.

Exercise 21

1. 次の各文を受動態に替えなさい．動作主が不要な場合は書かなくてよい．
1) Picasso drew the famous picture "Guernica" in 1937.
2) When did Thomas Edison invent the phonograph?
3) They released the CDs of the popular idol group the day before yesterday.
4) The high school baseball manager didn't select the lazy boy as a regular player.

2. 次の文の（　）に適当な前置詞を入れ，日本語に訳しなさい．
1) I was very surprised (　　　　) the big rolling in the earthquake.
2) She was disappointed (　　　　) the lecture about the care for the aged.
3) Dogs are pleased (　　　　) rubbing their backs.
4) Sakamoto Ryoma is known (　　　　) all Japanese people (　　　　) the greatest historical hero.

3. 次の受動文から能動文が作れるなら○，作れないなら×を書き，○の場合は能動文を書いてください．
1) Swahili is widely spoken in the eastern area of Africa.
2) His grandfather was killed in World War II.
3) We were very satisfied with the success of the college festival.
4) Nishikori Kei is now known to every tennis fan all over the world.

4. 次の日本文を英語に直しなさい．
1) これらのスナップ写真は卒業式のパーティーで撮ったものです．
2) その半島の先では，一風変わった方言が話されています．

3) その大学では環境保全に関する研究が盛んに行われています.

4) 君があんなことを言ったので，僕はとってもがっかりしました.

覚えておきたい英単語　21 和製英語のもとの英語

サラリーマン	office worker
サービス残業	unpaid overtime
クレーム	complaint
オーダーメイド	made-to-order
サイン（署名）	signature
ノートパソコン	laptop
（電気器具の）コンセント	outlet
（家の）リフォーム	redecoration / renovation
（喫茶店の）モーニングサービス	morning special
ホットケーキ	pancake
シュークリーム	cream puff
ペットボトル	plastic bottle
（部屋の）クーラー	air conditioner

第**22**章　使役構文

使役動詞の種類

「〜させる」という使役を表現する構文を**使役構文**（**causative sentence**）といい，使役構文に使われる動詞を**使役動詞**（**causative verb**）という．使役動詞には，make, let, have, get などがある．

I.　make

make O do（原形不定詞）の形で，「O に do させる」という意味の使役文を構成する．

Mr. Wilson **made** | his son | | go to his grandfather's house alone | .　……①
　　　　　　　　　　　O　　　　　　　　　　C

この使役文の構成を考えるとき，まず，目的語 O "his son" と，目的補語 C "go to his grandfather's house alone" の間に「主語—述語」の関係が成り立っていることに注目したい．つまり，① の OC の部分はさしずめ次のような文に書きかえ可能である．

His son went to his grandfather's house alone.　　　　　　　……②

そして，"make"「〜を作る」という他動詞の意味を考慮すると，意味の上での目的語は②の文で示される叙述内容全体であるといえる．つまり，①は「ウィルソン氏は②を作る（つまり「彼の息子が祖父の家に独りで行く」という状態を作る）」と解釈でき，①は③のように図示されうる．②の述語動詞 "went" は③では原形不定詞 "go" になり，②は③の中の | | のように変わる．

His son | went | to his grandfather's house alone. …②
　　　　　　　意味をなす叙述（主述関係あり）

Mr. Wilson | made | | his son | go | to his grandfather's house alone | . ……③
　　　　　　　　　　　　　　　　　　：意味の上での目的語

なお，make を使った使役文は受動態が可能である．その場合，原形不定詞は to 不定詞に替わる．

90

Ted was **made to go** to his grandfather's house alone.

II. let

let O do の形で「O に do させる」という意味の使役文を構成する．"make O do" は「強制的に～させる」という含みがあるのに対し，"let O do" は「自由に～させる」といった，許容，容認の含みがある．また，let を使った使役文には受動態はない．

In this kindergarten we **let the kids play** freely with wooden blocks.

III. have

have を使う使役文は，以下のような場合がある．いずれも使役動詞 have の受動態はない．

1) **have O do (原形不定詞)**：使役の意味とともに「～してもらう」という依頼の含みももつ．
   I **had the professor give** a lecture on the necessity of learning pronunciation in English education.

2) **have O doing (現在分詞)**：1) に加えて，「～するがままにさせる」「～しているのを許す」などのように，継続，進行中というニュアンスを与える．
   The police **had the public walking** safely on the broken road after the big earthquake hit the area.

3) **have O done (過去分詞)**：1), 2) に対して，O が補語の動詞の被動作主となる（つまり，受動の関係にある）場合，補語動詞は過去分詞になる．
   He **had his hair cut**.

この文は，"he" が例えば非常に高貴な人物で，cut の動作主に対して支配的である場合，「彼は髪を切らせた」となり，通常，理髪店でお願いするような場合は「彼は髪を切ってもらった」となる．もし，主語の "he" が迷惑あるいは被害を感じているならば，「彼は髪を切られた」となる．"have O done" は状況に応じて様々に訳し分けが可能である．

IV. get

"get" を使う場合は "have" を使う場合に準ずるが，上記の 1) に相当するのは "get O to do(to 不定詞)" である．

91

I **got a special mechanic to repair** the copy machine in our office.

知覚動詞の場合

視覚，聴覚などの知覚を表す動詞を**知覚動詞**（**verb of perception**）といい，知覚動詞を使った構文は使役文と同じ構文をとる．補語になる動詞は，have と同じく，原形不定詞，現在分詞，過去分詞のいずれもありうる．

According to the broadcast, the boy **saw a flying saucer float** above the mountain.

補語の動詞には，叙述の一部始終が含意される場合は原形不定詞，一瞬のできごとが関わる場合は現在分詞という目安はある．

I **saw a bird make** a nest.　　（一部始終を観察）

I **saw a bird making** a nest.　（一瞬見る）

また，受動態も可能である．その場合，make の使役構文と同じく，原形不定詞は to 不定詞に替わる．

The suspect **was seen to enter** the building.

 **22**

1. 次の文の（　）から適当なものを選びなさい.

1) Our school teacher made the rude student（clean / to clean / cleaning/）the restroom alone.

2) My mother didn't let me（play / to play / playing）outside after dark in my childhood.

3) A doctor gets patients（pay / to pay / paid）attention to their food.

4) We need to have this personal computer（repair / repairing / repaired）right now.

2. 次の英文を日本語に訳しなさい.

1) If there are any questions about the topic, please let me know at once.

2) When I was young I'd listen to the radio／Waitin' for my favorite songs／
   When they played I'd sing along, it made me smile.

   (The Carpenters: *Yesterday once more*)

3) In the evening, when it was getting dark, I saw an old lady staggering
   across the road. I was startled by her and put on the brakes of the car
   quickly.

4) We heard heavy rain fall severely.

3. 次の日本文を英語に訳しなさい.

1) 水族館の調教師が，アザラシに芸をさせています.

2) 僕は，小学校の時，遠足の作文を書かされたものでした.

3) 慎太郎は，列車が橋を渡りきるのをずっと見ていた.

4) アリスンは一人で歌っているのを聞かれてしまった.

覚えておきたい英単語 22 重要な形容詞・副詞

効果的な	effective
対称的な	symmetric
対照的な	contrastive
包括的な	comprehensive
個別の	individual
一般的に	generally
普遍的に	universally
個々に	respectively
部分的に	partially
公平に	fairly
偏りのある	biased
未決定の	pending
決定的な	crucial
致命的な	fatal

第23章　助動詞の表現

助動詞とは

　助動詞（**auxiliary verb**）とは，文字通りには「動詞を助ける品詞」（英語でも auxiliary →「補助となる」で「補助的動詞」と訳してよい）なので，形式的には，述語動詞に添えて用いるものはすべて助動詞である．通常は「助動詞」とは分類しないものに，**be**（be ＋現在分詞〈進行相〉，be ＋過去分詞〈受動態〉），**have**（have ＋過去分詞〈完了相〉），**do**（do ＋動詞原形〈疑問・否定・強調〉）がある．

　学校文法で学習してきたいわゆる「助動詞」とは，助動詞＋動詞原形 で表されるもので（上記 do は含まない），特に法助動詞（modal auxiliary）といわれるが，本章では単に「助動詞」と言及する．なお，本章では，上記 be, have, do は助動詞としては扱わない．

助動詞の意味

　文が単に事実を伝えている場合は，本動詞だけが使われるのに対し，助動詞を使った表現では，話し手もしくは文の主語の心理が表現されている．例えば，"He speaks English."「彼は英語を話す」という文に対して，

He can speak English.	「彼は英語を話すことができる」
He must speak English.	「彼は英語を話さなければならない」
He would speak English.	「彼は英語を話すだろう」
He might speak English.	「彼は英語を話すかもしれない」
He should speak English.	「彼は英語を話すべきである」
He had better speak English.	「彼は英語を話すほうがよい」

は，すべて話し手もしくは主語（この例では "he"）の心理が反映されているといえる．これが助動詞を用いる必要性である．

can, could

　can, could は，「～できる」という能力を付加する助動詞である．

Susanna can speak Japanese very well because she has lived in Japan for her studies.

could は can の過去形である．ただし，could には過去表現でない用法も多い．

過去： The legendary baseball player could throw a ball at a speed of 165km/h.
依頼・許可： Could you tell me the way to the station?

must, have to

must, have to は「～ねばならない」という義務の意味を付加する助動詞である．義務の程度は，must のほうが have to より強いとされる．

I must go home now.（別の用事があるので）
I have to go home now.（これ以上いると迷惑になるので）

must と have to の義務の程度の差は，否定文にしたときに反映される（must not（＞mustn't）：～してはならない，don't have to：～しなくてもよい）．

We mustn't speak ill of others.
Seniors over 65 don't have to pay entrance fee at this museum.

「～しなければならなかった」という過去の表現には must, have to いずれの場合も had to を使う．

We had to wait for a minute until it stopped raining.

must には「～に違いない」という推定の意味もある．この場合，過去の時間指示は must＋have＋過去分詞 の形をとる．

He must be tell a lie.
Jonathan must have caught the last train in time.

should

大まかには「～するべきである」という義務と「～するはずである」という当然の推量の表現の 2 種類がある．なお，過去の表現は should＋have＋過去分詞となる．

95

We should study a basic grammar for the practical use of English.

Tom should have left his mobile phone in the classroom.

would, might

形態的には would は will「〜だろう」の，might は may「〜するようだ」の過去形であるが，過去の時間表現のためにはほとんど使われない．それぞれ will, may の婉曲もしくは推量の程度が強く表現される．したがって，口語ではより丁寧な表現となる．

I would like to see your new house soon.

They might keep the matter secret.

would には，「過去の時点における未来」（未来形 [will + 動詞原形] の過去）を表現しうる．

At the point of yesterday the weather forecast said that it would be fine today.

Exercise 23

1. 次の各文の（　）に入る助動詞を下の [　] から選んで入れなさい（1 つだけ選択可）.

1) We (　　　) go home at once because it is getting dark.

2) He (　　　) swim fastest of all his classmates.

3) She (　　　) be French according to her sense of fashion.

4) I (　　　) like to invite him as a next lecturer in the symposium.

[can, might, must, would]

2. 次の各文に [　] の助動詞を加えて文を完成させなさい.

1) I don't visit her because she has been ill since last week.　[had better]

2) Do you mind turning down your iPod?　[would]

3) He met Betty yesterday.　[must]

4) Jimmy passed the entrance examination because he looks very happy now.

[should]

3. 次の英文を日本語に訳しなさい.

1) Anyone mustn't drive a car at a speed over 100km/h on an expressway.

2) I should have met Professor Suzuki when I went to Kobe last month.

3) Could you give your seat to me?

4) The suspect might have entered the building on the night of that day.

4. 次の日本文を英語に直しなさい.

1) 彼は迷子の飼い猫を見つけたに違いない.

2) 真理子は1時間に50ページの速さで本を読むことができる.

3) 明日は休みなので, 朝早く起きなくてもよい.

4) 彼のその冒険旅行は成功するかもしれないが, まず無理でしょう.

覚えておきたい 英単語

㉓ まぎらわしい綴りの組〈1〉

much	a. (量が) 多い
more	a. < many, much の比較級
except	prep. ～を除いて
expect	v. 予期する
quite	adv. 全く
quiet	a. 静かな
warm	a. 暖かい
worm	n. イモムシ
warn	v. 警告する
worn	v. < wear の過去分詞
wonder	v. 不思議がる
wander	v. 歩き回る

collect	v. 集める
correct	a. 正しい
saw	v. < see の過去形
sow	v. 種をまく
though	con. ～だけれど
thought	n. 考え
through	prep. ～を通って
thorough	a. 完全な
law	n. 法律
low	a. 低い
raw	a. 生の
row	n. 列

97

第24章 動詞の時制（2）

時制の基本

英語の仮定法を理解するうえで，時制はとても重要な概念であるので，もう一度この章で確認しておこう．

(1) The boy | bought | a birthday present for his sister.
「その少年は妹に誕生日プレゼントを買ってあげた.」

(2) The girl | knows | that dolphins are not fish.
「その少女はイルカが魚類でないことを知っている.」

(3) We | will go | out next Sunday.
「私たちは次の日曜日に外出するつもりです.」

上の (1)〜(3) では，動詞の時制はそれぞれ実際の出来事が生じる（生じた）時間に対応して，(1) 過去時制，(2) 現在時制，(3) 未来時制となっている．これを簡単な図式で表すと (4) のようになる.

(4)

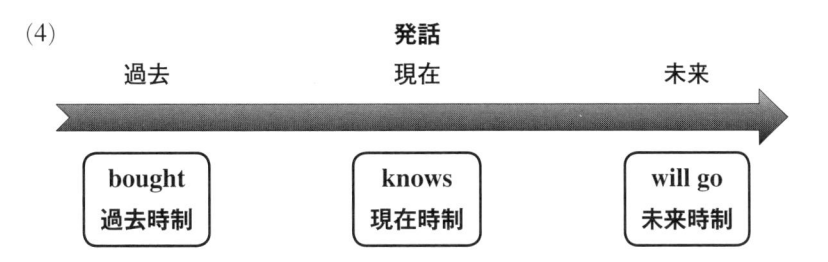

(4) では矢印の左から右に向かって，「過去」→「現在」→「未来」と時間が流れている．動詞の時制は，原則的には文が発話される「現在」を基準に決定される．発話時以前に生じた出来事であれば**過去時制**，発話時現在において生じている出来事であれば**現在時制**，発話時以降に生じる出来事であれば**未来時制**を用いる．このように動詞の時制は，基本的にその動詞が述べようとする出来事が現実の世界においてどの時間帯に生じるかに応じて決まる．しかしながら，実際には現実世界の出来事の生じる時間とそれを叙述する動詞の時制との間にずれが生じる場合がある．

未来を表す現在時制

英語では，未来に生じる出来事を現在時制で表すことがある．

(5) We ʼre having a meeting next Tuesday.
「私たちは来週火曜日に会議があります.」

(6) Your train leaves at 10 : 30.
「あなたの列車は 10 時 30 分に出発します.」

(7) I will wait here until he comes back.
「彼が戻ってくるまで，私はここで待ちます.」

まず，(5) は近い未来の計画（予定）を述べている文である．動詞は**現在時制（現在進行形）**となっているが，文が発話された現在において「会議が開かれている」のではない．この文には文末の時を表す副詞句 "next Tuesday" が発話時よりも未来の時間を指し示していることから，「会議の開催」は「未来」において生じる出来事となる．つまり，現在時制で未来の出来事を述べていることになり，動詞の時制と現実世界で出来事が生じる時との間にずれが見られる．

次に，(6) は列車の出発時刻を述べている文であるが，この列車は文の発話時以降に出発することは明らかである．この文のように乗り物などの時刻表やイベントのプログラムなど確定している未来の予定や計画などを述べる際には，(5) と同様に動詞は現在時制となる．

最後に (7) を見てみよう．この文には主節と副詞節があるが，主節の動詞が未来時制である一方，副詞節の動詞 "comes" は現在時制となっている．(7) には未来の時を表す明示的な語句は存在していないが，(8) からも明らかなように主節と副詞節の 2 つの出来事の時間的な前後関係を考えると副詞節で述べられている出来事も未来において生じることになる．

(8)

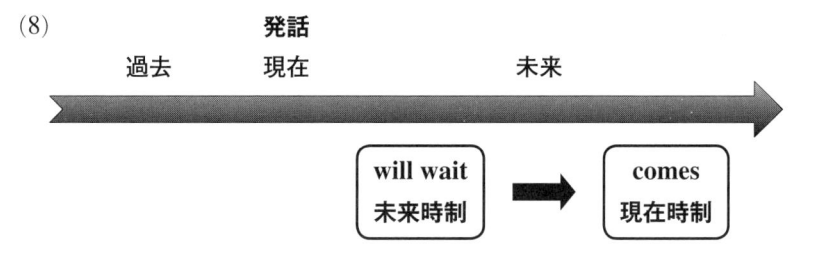

さらに未来における条件を述べる副詞節の動詞も現在時制となる．

(9)　If it rains tomorrow, the festival parade will be called off.
「明日雨が降れば，祭りのパレードは中止です.」

(9) の副詞節には未来を表す "tomorrow" があるが，動詞は未来時制 "will rain" とはならず，現在時制 "rains" となる.

以上のように英語では動詞の時制は基本的には現実世界の出来事が生じる時に対応しているが，特定の状況下では動詞の時制と現実の出来事の生じる時にずれが生じる．このことを頭にとどめたうえで，次章以降で**仮定法過去**と**仮定法過去完了**について確認していくことにする.

Exercise 24

1.　それぞれの文の [　] から適切な形を選びなさい.

1) My son [watches / is watching] TV every evening.

2) John [cooks / is cooking] dinner in the kitchen now.

3) [Are you knowing / Do you know] where he comes from?

4) My friend [doesn't / didn't] show up at the party last night.

5) My grandmother [lives / is living] in Hokkaido.

6) Lisa [goes / went] to the museum three days ago.

7) It was snowing when we [were leaving / left] the park.

8) Tom will be at home when you [visit / will visit] him.

9) I think Mike [accepts / will accept] the offer.

10) The last train [leaves / will leave] at 11:40.

2.　それぞれの文の動詞を適切な形にしなさい．一語とは限りません.

1) There (be) a lot of children in the park yesterday.

2) I (take) a bath when you phoned me.

3) My brother (clean) his room everyday.

4) Jack (start) marathon training four weeks ago.

5) I think Susan (attend) the ceremony tomorrow.

6) Kate (drink) coffee every morning.

7) She (be) born in 2006.

8) Turn off the lights before you (leave) the room.

9) I went to bed early last night because I (be) tired.

10) If she (feel) sick, she will not go out with us.

覚えておきたい
英単語 | **24** 同綴異義語

saw	[sɔ́ː]	v. < see の過去形
	〃	n. ノコギリ
sew	[sóʊ]	v. 縫う
	[súː]	v. 排水をする
sow	[sóʊ]	v. 種をまく
	[sáʊ]	n. 雌ブタ
row	[róʊ]	n. 列
	〃	v. 漕ぐ
lead	[líːd]	v. 導く
	[léd]	n. 鉛
found	[fáʊnd]	v. 設立する
	〃	v. < find の過去形・過去分詞
lie	[láɪ]	n. 嘘
	〃	v. 横になる

第25章　仮定法（1）

条件を表す副詞節

前章では，英語において未来に生じる出来事を，動詞の現在時制で述べることができることをみた．未来の条件を表す副詞節の動詞は現在時制であるが，現在と過去の条件を表す副詞節については，その動詞はそれぞれ現在時制と過去時制となり，実際の出来事が生じる時間と対応している．

(1)　If you talked with Sara, tell me what she said.
　　　「サラと話したのなら，彼女が話したことを教えてください.」

(2)　You have a good view of the ocean if you go upstairs.
　　　「二階に上がると素敵な海の景色が見えますよ.」

(3)　If it rains tomorrow, the festival parade will be called off.
　　　「明日雨が降れば，祭りのパレードは中止になります.」

(4)

過去	発話 現在	未来
talked 過去時制	**go** 現在時制	**rains** 現在時制

　(1)～(3)の副詞節はいずれも状況が整ったり，本人の意志が働いたりすることで，実現可能な条件を述べている．例えば，(2)では"you"は二階に上がることが許される状況にいて，"you"が二階に上がることを選択すれば，現実に二階に上がるという出来事が生じることになる．

　これに対して，日常生活の中では現実には生じていない出来事（事実とは逆の出来事）を話題にすることができる．そこでまず，次の日本語の文の表す意味を考えてみよう．

(5)　「私があなたなら，そんなことで腹を立てたりしない.」

　(5)は，単に「私はそんなことで腹を立てない」ということを述べているだけではなく，現実世界において「あなたがそんなことで腹を立てる」という出

102

来事が生じており，さらにはそのことが「私には驚きだ」というような話者の気持ちをも間接的に表すことができる．特に「私があなたなら」という条件を表す表現については，現実には「私」は「あなた」にはなれない（正確には「あなたの立場にいない」）のであるが，文としてはごく自然な表現である．英語においてもこのように事実とは異なる状況や条件を述べることができるが，ここで**仮定法**（**subjunctive mood**）が用いられることになる．

仮定法過去

(5) の日本語の文に対応する英文は次のようになる．

(6) If I were you, I wouldn't get angry about that.

(6) は主節の助動詞と条件を述べる副詞節の動詞はともに過去時制であるが，対応する日本語からも明らかなように現在の出来事について述べている文である．つまり，現実世界の出来事の生じる時間とその出来事を述べる動詞の時制との間にずれが生じている．未来の条件を述べる副詞節などにおいてもこのようなずれがあることはすでに確認しているとおりである．

(7)

	発話	
過去	現在	未来

were / wouldn't get
過去時制

このように現在の事実とは異なる（反する）状況について述べる仮定の状況や出来事を叙述する表現は**仮定法過去**（**subjunctive past**）と呼ばれる．他にいくつかの例を見てみよう．

(8) If I had time, I would travel abroad.
「時間があれば，海外旅行に行くのに．」
事実☞ 時間がなくて，海外旅行に行けない．

(9) If she weren't here, we would be in serious trouble.
「彼女がここにいなければ，大変困ったことになっているだろう．」
事実☞ 彼女がここにいてくれたので，困ったことにならなかった．

103

例文 (8), (9) からもわかるように**仮定法過去**では副詞節で現在の事実とは反対の仮定を述べ，その帰結として主節でも事実とは逆の事柄が述べられる．文脈によっては話者の希望や願望の意味が含まれることもある．

仮定法過去

If＋S＋ $\left\{ \begin{array}{l} \text{were} \\ \text{動詞の過去形} \end{array} \right\}$, S＋ $\left\{ \begin{array}{l} \text{would, could} \\ \text{might, should} \end{array} \right\}$ ＋動詞の原形

もし〜であれば，…するだろうに．

仮定法過去の特徴の 1 つとして，副詞節の動詞が be 動詞の場合，主語の数・人称にかかわらず "were" となることが挙げられる．ただし，口語では主語が一，三人称単数であれば "was" も使われることもある．

Exercise 25

1. それぞれの文の [　] から適切な形を選びなさい．
1) When I [see / saw] Chris, he looked well.
2) Don't drive if you [drink / drank].
3) If you [have / will have] a camera to the zoo, you can take pictures of animals.
4) I was 13 when I [move / moved] to this town.
5) If the suit [isn't / weren't] so expensive, I could buy it.
6) If you [leave / left] right now, you will catch up with her.
7) Ann would tell the truth if she [knows / knew] it.
8) This room [was / would be] brighter if it had a larger window.
9) I will wait here until it [stops / will stop] raining.
10) If the waves weren't so high, we [can / could] go swimming to the sea.

2. それぞれの文の (　) の動詞を適切な形にしなさい．1 語とは限りません．また，各英文を日本語に訳しなさい．
1) If you (take) this medicine, you will get well soon.

104

2) We will have a short break after we (finish) this job.

3) If she (be) here, she would be happy to meet you.

4) If the restaurant is closed, we (miss) lunch.

5) If you (install) this software, your computer will be protected.

3. 2つの文が同じ意味になるように空所に語句を入れなさい.

1) It is raining, so we can't see the other shore.

If it were not raining, we _____ the other shore.

2) I like that bag, but it's too expensive.

I _____ buy that bag if it _____ so expensive.

3) These shelves are too small to hold all these books.

If these shelves _____ so small, they _____ all these books.

4) I don't have a camera, so I can't take pictures of this beautiful scenery.

If I _____ a camera, I _____ pictures of this beautiful scenery.

5) The weather is bad, so few people are coming to the festival.

If the weather _____ better, many people _____ to the festival.

覚えておきたい
英単語　**25** 対義語の対

主観的	subjective	↔	客観的	objective
抽象的	abstract	↔	具体的	concrete
楽観的	optimistic	↔	悲観的	pessimistic
静的	static	↔	動的	dynamic
基礎的	basic	↔	応用的	applied
理論的	theoretical	↔	実践的	practical
懐疑的	skeptical	↔	独断的	dogmatic
帰納的	inductive	↔	演繹的	deductive
必然的	inevitable	↔	蓋然的	probable
感情的	emotional	↔	理性的	rational
総合的	synthetic	↔	分析的	analytic

105

第26章　仮定法（2）

仮定法過去完了

　前章では**仮定法過去**によって現在の事実とは異なる（反する）出来事について述べることができることをみた．それでは過去の事実とは異なる出来事について述べるにはどうすればよいのだろうか．

　ここで，過去のある時点よりもさらに過去の時点までの出来事（動作や状態の完了や経験など）を述べるために英語では**過去完了**が用いられることを思い出そう．

(1)　When I arrived at the station, the last train had already left .
　　「私が駅に到着した時には，最終電車はすでに出発していた．」

　(1) では主節の「電車が出発した」という出来事は，時を表す副詞節の「私が駅に到着した」という出来事よりもさらにさかのぼった過去において生じており，英語ではその時間の差を表すために**過去完了**が使われる．

(2)　**過去完了の時間軸**

発話

　　　　　　　過去　　　　　現在　　　　　　未来

| had left
過去完了 | | arrived
過去時制 | |

過去時制で表される出来事よりもさらに過去

　(2) からも分かるように**過去完了**は**過去時制**で表される出来事から見てさらに過去の時間帯において生じている出来事について述べている．

　それではこの**過去時制**と**過去完了**の関係を仮定法に当てはめてみたいと思う．**仮定法過去**が現在の出来事について過去時制を用いて述べるのであれば，仮定法において過去の出来事について，つまり**過去時制**で表される現在よりも過去の出来事を述べるには**過去完了**が使われることが予想される．英語では実際にそうした関係が成り立ち，仮定法において過去の出来事を表す文は**仮定法**

106

過去完了（**subjunctive past perfect**）と呼ばれている.

(3) **仮定法の時間軸**

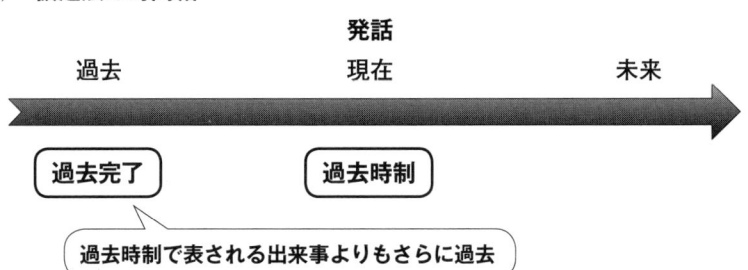

(4) If I ̲h̲a̲d̲ ̲s̲t̲u̲d̲i̲e̲d̲ much harder, I ̲w̲o̲u̲l̲d̲ ̲h̲a̲v̲e̲ ̲p̲a̲s̲s̲e̲d̲ the exam.
「もっと勉強していれば, 試験に受かったのに.」
事実☞ あまり勉強しなかったので, 試験に受からなかった.

(5) If you ̲h̲a̲d̲n̲'̲t̲ ̲g̲o̲n̲e̲ there, you ̲c̲o̲u̲l̲d̲n̲'̲t̲ ̲h̲a̲v̲e̲ ̲g̲o̲t̲ your present job.
「もしあそこへ行かなければ,あなたは現在の職を得ることはできなかっ
ただろう.」
事実☞ あそこへ行ったので, あなたは現在の職を得ることができた.

(4) と (5) はともに過去の事実とは反対の出来事を述べている文であり, 次の
ように図示されうる.

> **仮定法過去完了**
>
> If＋S＋had＋過去分詞, S＋$\begin{cases} \text{would, could} \\ \text{might, should} \end{cases}$＋have＋過去分詞
>
> もし～であったならば, …だっただろうに.

■ if 節に相当する表現

仮定法には if 節を伴わない文や慣用表現がある.

・Without ～：～がなければ

(6) Without the map, I would get lost.

・But for ～：～がなかったら

(7) But for your help, the experiment would have failed.

107

・I wish ～：～だったらなあ

(8) I wish I could speak Spanish.

(6) では「地図がない」ことを想定しているが実際には「地図を持っていて迷子にならなかった」，(7) では，現実の世界では「あなたの手助けはあって，実験は成功した」，(8) では wish 以下の節 "I could speak Spanish" は実際には実現していない，という意味で，いずれも非現実を表現する仮定法の表現として if 節と同等とみなせるのである．

(6) と (7) は事物の不在や出来事が生じないことを仮定する表現であるが，ともに If 節を用いた慣用表現で表すこともできる．この場合，通常は If 節内の be 動詞は主節の動詞の時制に合わせることになる．

(9) **If it were not for** the map, I would get lost.

(10) **If it had not been for** your help, the experiment would have failed .

Exercise 26

1. ( ) 内の動詞を適切な形にしなさい．ただし，1 語とは限らず，形が変わらないものもある．

1) After I finished my work, I (eat) dinner.

2) If Jim (be) there, he would have given me some advice.

3) When I woke up, my mother (go) to work.

4) If I (live) near the sea, I would go fishing every day.

5) When I (meet) Emily, she looked very tired.

6) If you (submit) all the assignments, you will get the credit.

7) If she (have) time tomorrow, she will go mountain climbing.

8) The girl sang as if she (be) a professional singer.

9) If you had made a reservation, you (can get) a good seat.

10) If we (purchase) that company, we wouldn't have been in a financial crisis.

2. 語句を並べ替えて英文を完成させなさい．

1) I [could / see the future / wish / I].

2) If [for / this key / were / it / not], you couldn't enter the room.

3) If [not / it / the train delay / been / for / had], I could have attended the meeting on time.

4) [financial support / for / but], the residents could not have recovered from the disaster.

5) If you had worn more clothes, you [caught / have / not / would / a cold].

3. 文 a を仮定法を使用した文 b に書き換えなさい.

1) a. He has enough money, so he will buy a car.

   b. If it _____ .

2) a. She stayed up late last night, so she was late for school.

   b. If she _____ .

3) a. I want to travel through time.

   b. I wish _____ .

4) a. I didn't go to the party, so I couldn't meet my old friends.

   b. If I _____ .

5) a. You did the reading assignments, so you could understand today's lecture better.

   b. If you _____ .

覚えておきたい英単語 **26 同音異義語**

[méɪl]	mail	n. 郵便
	male	n. 男性, 雄
[bíːt]	beat	v. 叩く
	beet	n. テンサイ, ビート
[bíːtʃ]	beach	n. 海岸
	beech	n. ブナ
[téɪl]	tail	n. しっぽ
	tale	n. 物語
[kάmpləmənt]	complement	n. 補完, 補語
	compliment	n. お世辞, 愛想
[prínsəpl]	principle	n. 原理
	principal	n. 社長, 校長

第27章　話法

話法を理解するための基礎知識

人の言葉を，" "（引用符）を使ってそのまま伝える形を**直接話法**（**direct narration**），引用符を使わないで伝える形を**間接話法**（**indirect narration**）という．

直接話法：　He said to me, "I will go here tomorrow."

間接話法：　He told me that he would go there the next day.

直接話法ではカンマ（,）によって前後の文が区切られているため，カンマの前の部分の時制が引用文に影響することはないが，間接話法の場合，接続詞を用いて1つの文になるため，カンマの前の部分の時制が過去形だった場合，時制の一致を受けて引用文の時制が**1つ前の時制にずれる**．また，それに伴い引用文中の時間と場所を表す表現が置き換えられる．ただし，**時制の一致の例外**があることに注意すること．

時制の一致を受けた場合の引用文の時制

直接話法の時	→	間接話法の時
現在形	→	過去形
現在進行形	→	過去進行形
現在完了形	→	過去完了形
過去形	→	過去完了形
過去進行形	→	過去完了進行形
過去完了形	→	過去完了形

時や場所を示す語句の置き換え

直接話法の時	→	間接話法の時
today	→	that day
tomorrow	→	the next day
yesterday	→	the day before
now	→	then
last night	→	the night before
ago	→	before
here	→	there
this	→	that

直接話法 → 間接話法への転換

He said to me, "I can swim now."

<u>伝達動詞</u>　　　　　<u>被伝達部</u>

110

上の文において，カンマの前に当たる部分の動詞を**伝達動詞**（**reporting verb**），引用文を**被伝達部**（**reported clause**）という．直接話法から間接話法への転換の際は，直接話法の被伝達部の文の種類によって使われる**公式**が変わる．

① 被伝達部が平叙文の場合

	直接話法	→	間接話法
伝達動詞	said to（said だけでは×）	→	told
被伝達部	"S＋V 〜"	→	that＋S＋V 〜

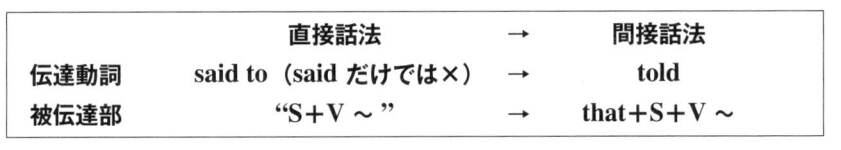

直接話法：He said to his father, " I want my own car now ."

間接話法：He told his father that he wanted his own car then .

　話法転換の際に注意すべき点は時制，時や場所を示す語句の置き換えの他に代名詞があり，直接話法の被伝達部の " I " や " my " は，間接話法に転換する場合，話し手である " he " に合わせなければならなくなるため，" I → he "，" my → his " に置き換えなければならない．また，"now" は "then" に換わる．

② 被伝達部が yes-no 疑問文の場合

	直接話法	→	間接話法
伝達動詞	said (to)	→	asked
被伝達部	"yes-no 疑問文"	→	if/whether＋S＋V 〜

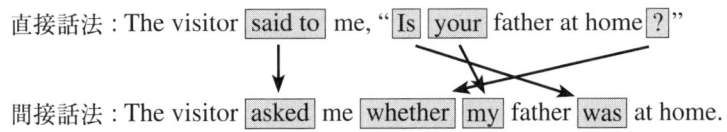

直接話法：The visitor said to me, " Is your father at home ? "

間接話法：The visitor asked me whether my father was at home.

直接話法の被伝達部の "your" は，間接話法に転換する場合聞き手に相当するので，"your → my" に置き換える．また間接話法の被伝達部は，語順が**疑問文ではなく平叙文の語順になる**ことに注意.

③ 被伝達部が wh 疑問文の場合

	直接話法	→	間接話法
伝達動詞	said (to)	→	asked
被伝達部	"wh 疑問文"	→	wh 疑問詞＋S＋V 〜

111

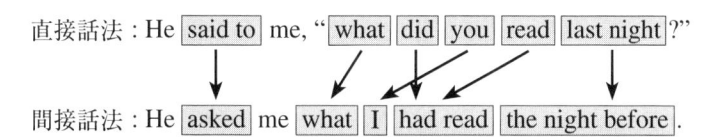

直接話法の被伝達部が wh 疑問文の場合，間接話法の被伝達部はいわゆる間接疑問文の語順になる．

④ 被伝達部が命令文，依頼・忠告を意味する文の場合

	直接話法	→	間接話法	
伝達動詞	said（to）	→	命令文	told
			依頼文	asked
			忠告の意味	advised
被伝達部	命令・依頼・忠告の意味の "肯定文" →			to 不定詞
	命令・依頼・忠告の意味の "否定文" →			not＋to 不定詞

直接話法：He said to me, "Don't leave your bag open."

間接話法：He advised me not to leave my bag open.

この場合は，直接話法の被伝達部の意味の種類によって間接話法の**伝達動詞が異なる**ので注意が必要である．

⑤ 被伝達部が Let's ～ の場合

	直接話法	→	間接話法
伝達動詞	said（to）	→	suggested（to）または proposed（to）
被伝達部	"Let's ～ "	→	that＋we＋(should)＋動詞の原形 ～

直接話法：He said to me, "Let's play tennis at this tennis court."

間接話法：He suggested to me that we (should) play tennis at that tennis court.

間接話法の被伝達部にある "should" は省略ができる．

112

Exercise 27

1. 次の英文を，間接話法を用いた文に書き換えなさい.

1) I said to her, "Where did you go last night?"

2) He said to me, "Could you show me the way to the station?"

3) Tom said to her, "You had better finish your homework."

4) He said to me, "Are you going there by train?"

5) He said to us, "Let's talk about the plan."

6) He said to me, "I want to drink a cup of tea."

7) The man said, "There was a theater here ten years ago."

覚えておきたい
英単語　　**27** まぎらわしい綴りの組〈2〉

lawn	n. 芝	direct	a. 直接の	
loan	n. 貸し付け, ローン	dialect	n. 方言	
celebrate	v. 祝う	globe	n. 地球	
cerebral	a. 大脳の	glove	n. 手袋	
lecture	n. 講義, 講演	grove	n. 木立	
rectangle	n. 長方形	valency	n. 結合価	
sensible	a. 分別のある	variety	n. 多様性	
sensitive	a. 感じやすい, 敏感な	balance	n. つりあい	
seem	v. 〜のようである	bat	n. 野球のバット, 蝙蝠	
seen	v. < see の過去分詞	bad	a. 悪い	
considerate	a. 思いやりのある	but	con. しかし	
considerable	a. かなりの	bud	n. 蕾	

113

第**28**章　まとめ（2）　5文型

　文は述語動詞の性質によって5つの文型に分けることができる．この5文型を理解することは，文の構造を理解することでもあり，英文を読んで理解し，そして正確な英語を書くために非常に重要である．

文型の基本

　文型は**主語**（**subject: S**），**動詞**（**verb: V**），**目的語**（**object: O**），**補語**（**complement: C**）の4つの要素から構成される．動詞は**自動詞**（**intransitive verb**）と**他動詞**（**transitive verb**）に分けることができる．また目的語は日本語で主に「〜を」と訳される**直接目的語**（**direct object: DO**）と，主に「〜に」と訳される**間接目的語**（**indirect object: IO**）とに分けられる．

文型の種類

＜第1文型＞　主語＋自動詞（S＋V）

　<u>My brother</u> <u>talks</u> fast.
　　　　S　　　　　　V

　第1文型で用いられる動詞は自動詞で，主語が何かを行うことで文が成り立ち，fast は副詞で修飾語として扱われ，文の要素にならない.

　<u>Ken</u> often <u>looks</u> at the sky.
　　S　　　　　V

この文は動作（look）の対象（the sky）が示されているが，look が自動詞であるために at という前置詞を必要とする．主語になるのは名詞，代名詞あるいは動名詞などである．

＜第2文型＞　主語＋自動詞＋補語（S＋V＋C）

　<u>Rumiko</u> <u>is</u> <u>the student</u> at A University.
　　　S　　　V　　　　C

　第2文型で用いられる動詞は自動詞で，主語について補足説明する主格補語と呼ばれる補語を伴う．Rumiko＝the student であるので，S＝C の関係が成り立つ．第2文型によく用いられる動詞は be 動詞，become, get, keep, look 等で，補語になるのは名詞，形容詞，分詞，名詞節などがある．

She became interested in modern art.
S V C

Keep going until your dream comes true.
V C

The problem is whether we have enough money or not.
S V   C

＜第3文型＞　主語＋他動詞＋目的語 (S＋V＋O)

I have a brother.
S V O

第3文型は目的語を取る他動詞を使う文で，主語が行う動作の対象は目的語として示される．V をはさんだ2つの要素について，第2文型は S＝C であるのに対して，第3文型は S≠O である．目的語になるのは名詞，代名詞，動名詞，名詞句，名詞節である．

I know that Kumi is from Osaka.
S V   O

I don't know if she will come or not.
S V   O

「～するのが好きだ」の意味では，like の目的語に動名詞，to 不定詞のどちらを用いてもよい．

I like swimming in the river.
I like to swim in the river.

＜第4文型＞　主語＋他動詞＋間接目的語＋直接目的語 (S＋V＋IO＋DO)

I will show you the way to the station.
S V IO   DO

第4文型は他動詞の後に直接目的語と間接目的語の2つの目的語を取る．直接目的語は基本的に人に準ずるもの，間接目的語は物に準ずるものが置かれ，名詞句や名詞節が来ることもある．

Please tell me what to do with this situation.
    V IO   DO

We asked our teacher when the test would start.
S   V   IO   DO

第 4 文型の文は次のように，第 3 文型に書き換えることが可能である．

My teacher gave us a lot of assignments.　（第 4 文型）
S   V IO   DO

My teacher gave a lot of assignments to us.　（第 3 文型）
S   V   O

＜第 5 文型＞　主語＋他動詞＋目的語＋補語（S＋V＋O＋C）

I found the book very interesting.
S V   O   C

　第 5 文型は他動詞の次に目的語とその目的語を補足説明する目的格補語がくる．第 5 文型では book＝interesting すなわち O＝C の関係が成り立つが，第 4 文型では IO≠DO である．補語には名詞，形容詞，現在分詞，過去分詞，不定詞が置かれる．

We named our daughter *Misaki*.
S   V   O   C

I made my sister the vice president.
S V   O   C

I heard David crying in his room.
S V   O   C

It is difficult to make ourselves understood.
           V   O   C

Exercise 28

1.　次の 1）〜 10）の英文中の下線部の動詞は，下の ① 〜 ⑤ の英文中のどの動詞と働きや性質が似ているか ① 〜 ⑤ の番号で答えなさい．

　① I come from Osaka.　② I am a student.　③ I have a pen.

　④ I gave you a call.　⑤ I will let you know soon.

116

1) The earthquake happened last year.

2) I believe he is an honest man.

3) My mother wants to climb that mountain.

4) The movie sounds interesting.

5) The student made me angry.

6) Mikiko brought me the umbrella.

7) It is difficult to talk about the issue.

8) The company gave you a chance to go abroad.

9) I had my hair cut yesterday.

10) I spoke to three different teachers this morning.

2. 各文型の文を1つずつ書きなさい.

第1文型：　　　　　　　　　第2文型：

第3文型：　　　　　　　　　第4文型：

第5文型：

覚えておきたい英単語

㉘ まぎらわしい綴りの組〈3〉

┌ break	v. 破る，砕く		┌ die	v. 死ぬ
└ brake	n. ブレーキ		└ dye	v. 染める
┌ electric	a. 電気の		┌ diner	n. 食堂
└ electronic	a. 電子の		└ dinner	n. 夕食
┌ intellectual	a. 知的な，知性の		┌ personal	n. 個人の
└ intelligent	a. 聡明な		└ personnel	n. 人事課，全職員
┌ divide	v. 分割する		┌ label	n. 貼り紙，ラベル
└ devise	v. 工夫する		level	n. 高さ，レベル
┌ carrier	n. 運搬車		└ rebel	n. 反逆者
└ career	n. 経歴，生涯		┌ participate	v. 参加する
┌ elect	v. 選ぶ		participle	n. 分詞
└ erect	v. 立てる		└ particle	n. 小辞，小片

117

執筆者紹介

【編集・執筆】
桑本　裕二（くわもと・ゆうじ）《執筆担当 1, 2, 3, 4, 20, 21, 22, 23 章》

1968 年鳥取県生まれ．東北大学大学院文学研究科博士後期課程修了．博士（文学）．専門は言語学，特に音韻論．一関工業高等専門学校非常勤講師，秋田工業高等専門学校准教授等を経て，公立鳥取環境大学教授．主要著書『改訂版　小学校英語　発音のフシギ』（2017 年，秋田魁新報社）．英語教育に対しては，発音と文法養成の重要性を説く．

【執筆】
菅原　隆行（すがわら・たかゆき）《執筆担当 11, 12, 13, 27 章》

1970 年宮城県生まれ．東北大学大学院情報科学研究科博士後期課程修了．博士（情報科学）．専門は英語学，特に統語論．秋田工業高等専門学校准教授．主要業績 Licensing of Parasitic Gaps（2000 年，*Papers from the Seventeenth National Conference of The English Linguistic Society of Japan*）．英語教育に関しては，文法力を活かした英文の精読を重要視している．

中村　弘子（なかむら・ひろこ）《執筆担当 14, 15, 16, 28 章》

1961 年大阪府生まれ．神戸市外国語大学大学院外国語学研究科修士課程（英語学），及び米国コネチカット大学修士課程コミュニケーション・サイエンス研究科修了．文学修士．M.A.　専門は英語教育，言語障害．帝塚山短期大学，大阪外国語大学非常勤講師等を経て，公立鳥取環境大学准教授．主要著書『ことばの認知のしくみ』（2007 年，三省堂，分担執筆）．英語教育に関してはプロソディの習得を重視している．

二本柳　譲治（にほんやなぎ・じょうじ）《執筆担当 7, 8, 9, 19 章》

1965 年岩手県生まれ．東北大学大学院文学研究科博士後期課程退学．文学修士．専門は言語学，特にラテン語学．一関工業高等専門学校准教授．英語教育に関しては，語彙を歴史的・文化的に取り扱うことの重要性を説く．

福士　智哉（ふくし・ともや）《執筆担当 5, 6, 17, 18 章》

1973 年青森県生まれ．函館工業高等専門学校機械工学科卒．東北大学大学院文学研究科博士後期課程退学．修士（文学）．専門は言語学，特に音韻論．大分工業高等専門学校講師等を経て，木更津工業高等専門学校助教．主要業績 Stress on Pretonic Light Syllable in English Affixed Words（2003 年，東北大学言語学論集第 12 号）英語教育に関しては，論理的思考を重視した英語による情報検索能力の向上とその重要性を説く．

福光　優一郎（ふくみつ・ゆういちろう）《執筆担当 10, 24, 25, 26 章》

1976 年鳥取県生まれ．東北大学大学院文学研究科博士後期課程退学．修士（文学）．専門は言語学，特に統語論．新居浜工業高等専門学校准教授．主要業績 Covert Incorporation of Small Clause Predicates in Japanese（2001 年，*MIT Working Papers in Linguistics 41*）．英語教育に関しては恒常的なアウトプット練習の重要性を説く．

大学・高専・短大生のための
英文法再入門

ISBN978-4-7589-2312-5　C3082

監修者	桑本裕二
著作者	桑本裕二・菅原隆行・中村弘子・二本柳譲治・
	福士智哉・福光優一郎
発行者	武村哲司
印刷所	日之出印刷株式会社

2019 年 3 月 5 日　第 1 版第 1 刷発行 ©

発行所	株式会社　開 拓 社	〒 113-0023 東京都文京区向丘 1-5-2 電話　(03) 5842-8900（代表） 振替　00160-8-39587 http://www.kaitakusha.co.jp

JCOPY ＜出版者著作権管理機構 委託出版物＞

本書の無断複製は，著作権法上での例外を除き禁じられています．複製される場合は，そのつど事前に，出版者著作権管理機構（電話 03-3513-6969，FAX 03-3513-6979，e-mail: info@jcopy.or.jp）の許諾を得てください．